W.& A.K.Johnston. Limited. Edinburgh.& London

PRINTED IN GREAT BRITAIN
BY WESTERN PRINTING SERVICES LTD. BRISTOL
FOR CHRISTOPHER JOHNSON PUBLISHERS LTD.
FIRST PUBLISHED 1948

S. P. B. MAIS

I RETURN TO SWITZERLAND

WITH 48 PLATES
INCLUDING NUMEROUS PHOTOGRAPHS
BY THE AUTHOR

Ruth Bayley. '40

CHRISTOPHER JOHNSON LONDON

CONTENTS

TO
MY
THREE
GRAND
COMPANIONS
IMOGEN
LALAGE
and
GILLIAN
to whom
I
OWE
my
LIFE'S
HAPPINESS
with all my
LOVE

MÜRREN–WENGEN: 1922–4

"SKIING," said Arnold Lunn, "is not what it was in our day."

That was on the overcrowded boat coming home in April 1947.

As I owe my introduction to and love of Switzerland entirely to Arnold Lunn perhaps I'd better explain who he is.

I have met in my long and singularly varied life three Titans, and only three.

These were (in order of my meeting them) the late "Skipper" Lynam, founder of the Dragon, by far the largest, the most flourishing (and I think the best) preparatory school in this country and therefore in the world, the late Charles ("Chas") Lowry, my headmaster at Tonbridge, and R. D. Blumenfeld, "R.D.B." to Fleet Street, my chief when I was on the staff of the *Daily Express*.

It is not, I think, altogether because all these three men knocked me down for three very different expressions of opinion (though this may be an important factor) that I place them on a pedestal by themselves.

These three men had a tremendous zest for life. They knew what they were doing. They knew where they were going. They fired me with their own enthusiasm. They were not time-servers. Two of them moulded the characters of generations of boys and their influence is still alive in the schools where they taught, the third moulded the opinions of a vast mass of newspaper readers, many of whom were not easily malleable.

The *Daily Express* has built up an enviable reputation for being accurate, crisp, lively and entertaining. It owes these qualities to "R.D.B." and if you don't believe me turn up the back files and read the *Daily Express* in the days before "R.D.B." took it over.

Arnold Lunn is not a member of my holy trinity. If, however, he has not attained in my view the godhead he is a little higher than the angels. Most of my angels are women. He is an arch-angel, Lucifer. I admire him immensely on several grounds. I admire him as I admire Lucifer for his readiness to rebel. Like myself he has rebelled against almost everything in his time. He is one of those rare men who think for themselves. He was the son of a rebel, who was a devout Evangelical and medical mis-sionary in India (where Arnold, like another of my heroes, Kipling, was born), and the founder of a famous travel agency.

Arnold was educated at Harrow and wrote one of the very few honestly illuminating public-school stories about that strange foundation. The fact that he introduced a grotesque travesty of myself into that book (Quirk by name) is typical of Arnold. I expect only the unexpected from him. Even today he never answers my letters. I no longer read his books, but the fact that he has collaborated with the Right Reverend Monsignor Ronald Knox, Oxford's Catholic Chaplain, with Professor C. E. M. Joad (who is, I think, not a Catholic) and with Professor J. B. S. Haldane, who is a freethinker, proves, I think, that he is not hidebound in his religious views. He has also written a life of John Wesley. You may deduce what you like from that. I am not sure whether he is a Catholic, a freethinker, or a Nonconformist, but it seems to me pretty obvious that he is deeply interested in sectarianism, and I like a man to take a look at all the churches before he starts appraising any of them. " In My Father's house are many mansions."

What class he took in schools at Oxford I don't know. The fact that he was at Balliol gives no clue. I suspect a bad one, as he found time to be Secretary of the Union, and edit the *Isis*, which are perhaps more educative processes than attending lec-tures. I don't know how he lost the use of one leg. I've forgotten which leg it is. I know very little about my hero, except his inability to answer letters and his studied (is it studied?) rudeness to me whenever we meet. He thinks I can't write and says so. He thinks I've no brains and says so. His standards are high. He can write and his brain functions admirably. I mention his physi-cal disability because it is as important, in my view, as Milton's blindness.

Arnold Lunn taught me to ski. I am physically perfect. Shall

I throw in the fact that I am a Double Blue? I have seen many skilful skiers. Arnold on skis is like a gannet diving. He has never been rude to me about skiing. It isn't worth his while. I on skis am like an American G.I. on a bicycle. I have passed my third-class test. That took sweat, tears, and blood. I am not naturally clumsy. I am a graceful runner. I am not a graceful skier. I once went skiing down the Mohawk trail with two Americans from Schenectady. That was sixteen years ago. I shouldn't be surprised to hear that they are still laughing. I like skiing, just as I like cricket. My prowess is unequal to my zeal.

"If," says the hero of Frederic Wakeman's *The Hucksters*, "a thing isn't worth doing at all, it isn't worth doing well."

Skiing and cricket are so much worth while doing at all that it's very much worth while doing them even if you're as bad as I am. I learnt my skiing from the archangel of skiing in Mürren, the paradise of skiers. I am told that it is the hardest of ski-schools. As there was practically no snow when I learnt I can believe that.

I realise that I am being rather wordy, but I am trying to convey to you the fact that Arnold Lunn has courage, and if there is one quality that I hold in higher esteem than any other it is guts. Arnold has guts. He also has a very ready, if at times a too astringent, wit. I am one of his open-mouthed listeners. I do not as a rule listen patiently to my fellow countrymen. I have a dislike for clichés and platitudes that is almost as pronounced as my dislike of parsnips.

Arnold uses no clichés, never falls into platitudes.

He has—this is quite by the way—never grown up. He is still the owlish-looking precocious young Harrovian, or should I say son of Balliol?

He has never lost the way of speaking of the brilliant undergraduate of his vintage year. He had written a guide to Montana (nothing to do with Butte) before he was twenty. He is (in spite of his game leg) a member of the M.C.C.; he is, in spite of that leg, a member of the Alpine Club, and (with that brain) a member of the Conservative Club. He is, what I admire more than anything else in these socialist days, an aristocrat. He dares to stand for the best in religion, in sport, in aesthetics, and probably (because he lives in Switzerland) in manners, wine, and food.

A* 9

I have very seldom wanted to change places with any of my fellow men. I would change places with Shakespeare, with William Cobbett, and with Arnold Lunn. I share only one honour with him. I too have been on the Brains Trust. He was an outstanding success. It is unlikely that he will be invited again.

"Skiing," said Arnold Lunn (pronouncing the word as spelt), "is not what it was in our day."

My day was 1922–4.

I was on the staff of the *Daily Express*. "R.D.B." raised no objection to my taking my Christmas leave in Switzerland at that time as winter sports was news. I sent back a lot of stuff. I went out with the cameramen who were of course highly paid to take this holiday, but their job wasn't all jam. They had to hang around the entrances of the de luxe hotels in St. Moritz, waiting for the photogenic film stars and society debutantes to make their dazzling appearance in what are often astonishingly inappropriate clothes for ski-running. They don't as a rule ski. They are or look like models, the sort of girls who figure in the advertisements of *Vogue* and *Harper's*. They have something to sell and people buy it. It is a queer thing but not, I think, important that the Swiss air which keeps the Swiss people so astonishingly sober in their conduct goes straight to the Englishman's head and makes him perform the oddest antics without a trace of shame or self-consciousness. Perhaps readers of my subsequent pages will consider that the Swiss air had a heady effect on me. I don't know. I leave that to them.

I went out with Harold Balfour who had been a contemporary of mine at Cranwell, and we were both armed with the gold medal of the American Express Company, which meant that we got a free pass on the steamer and railways in return for imparting information to and looking after the interests of travellers who had booked their tour through that company. As neither of us spoke a word of French or German and as neither of us had made the journey before you might feel that more knowledgeable couriers would have been more appropriate. You would be wrong. Harold and I were both an unqualified success. We were honest about our ignorance, which tickled our clients, and we were friendly, and both our history and geography were a good deal in advance of those of the more experienced couriers who concentrated solely on such mundane things as customs and seats. We extolled the view and were quite ready to embark on explanations of the French and Swiss political systems. We earned our gold medals all right.

My first impression of Mürren at this distance of time is naturally blurred, but I remember being frightened by the funicular that runs up from Lauterbrunnen, because it made my nose bleed and my ears sing.

I was frightened of Mürren because it is perched right on the edge of a precipice and I expected it to be swept away by an avalanche. I was overawed by the mighty shapes across the valley of the Eiger, Mönch and Jungfrau. I have always had a deep love for hills, but with that love is mixed respect and awe. For the Jungfrau I felt a great deal of awe and not much love. It was too big, too high for me ever to get to know.

In Arnold's hotel, the Palace des Alpes, I met a gang of people for whom I soon felt more love and less respect. There was in particular a girl whose photograph I still treasure. We went to a fancy-dress ball together, she as a Hawaiian, dressed in bits of straw, and I as a Dutchman. The air of Switzerland certainly does something to the emotions. I have no idea what her name is. I doubt if I ever knew it, but we certainly did have fun. Indeed the mountain air has something. The whole hotel was just one riotous crazy gang led by that astonishingly versatile and witty artist Alan D'Egville, who skis as gracefully as a chamois leaps and is as full of quips and jests as Tommy Handley.

There was no withstanding D'Egville. He had the party just where he wanted it. If anybody began by trying to be aloof and standoffish he broke them down with the ease with which a hard frost breaks up the good earth. He would be worth a fortune to Butlin as a "hi-de-hi ho-de-ho" man.

In the train and across the Channel the Englishman regards his fellow traveller, whether fellow countryman or not, as Cain regarded Abel, and only looks for a chance to eliminate him. In Switzerland he regards her as Romeo regarded Juliet or (if it is a he) as Hamlet regarded Horatio. We fell shamelessly in love with all the comely women, and became friendly with members of our own sex that we should have run a mile from at home.

What delightful company they were.

I remember best Mary Hope Morley, Duff Taylor the skating

expert, the Schusters, Shaw Stewart, Geoffrey Dennis, Jim Pit-man, Chris Mackintosh, Ken Foster—a whole crowd who may have been just pleasant or even ordinary at home, but were to me all electrically exciting and lovable in Mürren.

I didn't spend more than an hour or two on the nursery slopes. I was anxious to try my wings. I sweated my guts out to pass my third-class test, 1,500 metres of climbing and 1,500 metres of descent in 1½ hours. It takes about 1 hour 28 minutes to climb and 2 minutes to ski down. In these days of ski hoists, ski lifts, and that fearsome ropeway at Champéry, nobody climbs. Life is all one downhill rush. You no longer have to earn your delight.

Arnold, Lady Mabel Lunn, and D'Egville took me out on a few expeditions, but it was like Olympic 100-metre athletes taking out a three-year-old child for a run. They whisked out of sight over a precipice and I christying, stemming, telemarking, and falling (mainly falling), followed them traversing down the slopes by way of a hundred hairpin bends. They skimmed through woods as if the trees were not there. Whenever I entered a wood I couldn't see the snow for the trees. What I don't know about the resilient qualities of Swiss bark is not worth knowing. I en-joyed moments of complete ecstasy when the others had gone out of sight and too far for me ever to hope to see them again. Then I would just stand in the hot sun and look out over the glittering snow to the great peaks, commune with my heart and be still. I then felt as never before the presence of the Invisible God. I felt a serenity and exhilaration of spirit that I have never felt at home.

It is essential to be alone to feel this, and they don't leave you alone much in Switzerland. The lonely skier is unpopular. It is easy to break a ski or for that matter a leg, and I've spent too much time in the black, ice-cold hours of the night searching the mountain slopes for lost skiers to regard the lonely skier with any-thing but disfavour. The lonely skier is a fool, and is like a dog that will try to dodge across the road in front of fast-moving cars to see a dog about another dog.

I spent all the sunny hours out of doors on skis. I spent many nocturnal hours luging under the light of the moon. I danced a great deal with my Hawaiian. I listened to Geoffrey Dennis, author of *Mary Lee* retailing what I was told were " quaint " limericks in Greek, Latin, Russian, Lithuanian, Polish, Esthonian, French, Italian, Spanish, Urdu, Chinese, Thibetan, and all the tongues of Babel.

I enjoyed myself so much that I wanted to stay in Mürren for ever.

Yet I never went back.

The following year I changed over to Wengen, which lies a little lower down than Mürren on the other side of the Lauterbrunnen valley. Mürren is about five thousand feet above sea level and Wengen about four thousand feet. Wengen is a gentler place altogether. Mürren is the hardest ski school in Switzerland, a sort of Chelsea Barracks; Mürren takes skiing very seriously. At Wengen skiing is just fun. Indeed I, who was regarded at Mürren as the lowest form of creeping life, rose rapidly in the category of living things at Wengen and was actually appointed to be judge of third-class tests. I even entered for a race and came in among the first hundred. The excursions from Mürren all bristled with difficulties, but it would be hard to find simpler or for that matter more enjoyable runs than those from the Scheidegg to Wengen, from the Scheidegg to Grindelwald and (best of all) from the top of the Männlichen to Grindelwald. Grindelwald is too shut in for my liking. I like the hills, but I don't like being shut in by hills. Sun is so rare in England that I feel cheated in Switzerland if I am not in its full glare every hour of every day.

Wengen is (or is this my imagination?) cheaper and a little more genial than Mürren. I think it is better situated because it is on the way to the Jungfraujoch and the famous Aletsch Glacier. It is, I know, greener. When Mürren has thirty inches of snow it is quite possible for Wengen to have a bare half-dozen.

But Wengen is nearer the Scheidegg, the rendezvous of all the world's skiers.

In those far-off days there was only the station hut. Today the hut has been replaced by a palatial hotel, from the balconies of which you can watch the avalanches roar down the mountainside and see chamois perched on distant crags.

One of the insoluble mysteries of my strange life is why I stayed away from Switzerland for twenty-five years having once given my heart to it. I still think skiing the most wonderful of all sensations so far as the propulsion of the human body through space is concerned.

It is quite impossible to exaggerate its thrills or the purity of the pleasure which it engenders. It has one supreme advantage over all other sports. You can be an expert skier almost as soon as you can walk and you can continue to be an expert skier till you are well over seventy. You can enjoy it equally well, or almost equally well, whether you can ski skilfully or clumsily. There is always something to learn.

In fairness, however, let me say that those people I met in Wengen who spent their whole time uttering bloodcurdling Highland battle-cries on the curling rink, pirouetting round the skating rink evolving more and more intricate mathematical figures, skijoring along the roads behind jingling horse-sleighs, flying down the luge-runs, or just messing about the shops or drinking in the sun, all appeared to be getting as much of a kick out of life as we one-track-minded skiers got.

The point is, I think, that whatever your frivolous occupation Switzerland intoxicates you.

I RETURN TO SWITZERLAND: 1947

My determination to return to Switzerland after an absence of twenty-five years was undoubtedly due to my refusal ever to contemplate the possibility of a repetition of the fiasco of last summer holidays.

I took the family to (of all places) Ilfracombe. My intention had been to return to Woolacombe, our usual summer holiday resort before the war. As Woolacombe was in the throes of a paratyphoid epidemic or scare we were advised to avoid it. Ilfracombe was near. That was one recommendation. Ilfracombe was the only resort in the British Isles with any accommodation left. That was also a recommendation.

We went to Ilfracombe, which surely bears the palm for man-made ugliness and vulgarity even in these islands. It rained every day for six weeks. It blew every day for six weeks. Even a pleasant resort might prove distasteful in such circumstances. Ilfracombe is not a pleasant place for children. There are no sands. There is not a single yard of level ground on which to play cricket or rounders. My family were models of patience. I was a model of frustration and irritability.

We were charged ten guineas a week per head, and given dirty plates and cutlery, ill-cooked, unimaginative, and insufficient food. There was plenty in two directions—in rudeness from the shop assistants, Welsh waitresses, chambermaids, and bus conductors, and in the number of people queuing up for cinemas, apples, seats at the draughty Alexandra Hall for what were euphemistically called theatrical performances, for buses, for motor-coaches, and for ices—most of all for ices. It was almost the only form of food available.

The experience cost me £300 and it was experience bought

dear. I do not propose to repeat it. Nor, I think, do about two hundred thousand deluded holiday-makers who set out at all costs to enjoy Ilfracombe and failed. They failed patiently. I failed impatiently. I have never been so glad to get home. I have never been called upon before to pay so much for so little or to endure such discomfort and discourtesy. You can keep all the large, popular English seaside resorts, except Brighton, for me. You can also keep the English summer weather.

I began to cast around for some place where we might recover from this worse than no holiday.

I thought of Switzerland. I thought of Arnold Lunn. I wrote to Arnold Lunn. Characteristically I got no reply from Arnold Lunn.

I went to Eccleston Square to call on Mr Brown, the Director.

He was most helpful.

I suggested Villars at Christmas. He told me that there wasn't a vacant room in all Switzerland for Christmas.

"I might get you in at Montreux at Easter."

"Easter?" I echoed contemptuously. "Who could ever want to go to Montreux at Easter?"

"You'll be surprised," he said.

I might as well confess now that I was surprised.

But there was a long time to go and a lot to do.

He began by asking for passports. Mine were long out of date. Passports, however, seemed easy to renew. He began to talk about money and hotels. He recommended two hotels. I chose the less expensive, the Bonivard.

The inclusive charge for the journey and the hotel for each grown-up for sixteen days was £30. After Ilfracombe that struck me as reasonable. The charges for the children were less. That struck me as equally reasonable.

He began to juggle with figures. Apparently I was to be allowed to spend £230 for the four of us (£75, £75, £40 and £40) of which £120 was deducted for the hotel bill. It seemed enough.

It was, just.

As the English winter gave us its grand slam I began to fear that we should not live through it to escape to the Delectable Land.

It seemed much too good to be true. I couldn't believe that we were really going to Switzerland at last.

But God was very good. We did go. And this is what happened.

Wednesday, 9th April, 1947

AT long last the great day dawned. After sixteen weeks of unprecedented hard frost (with accompanying burst pipes, treacherous roads, unbelievable cold, and all the rest), gales which blew my fences down, my windows out, and felled a tall fir in my garden, floods which marooned Oxford as an island, and a sky which never for a single day permitted the sun to shine, we were free to escape.

I had never felt the need of sun and blue skies more.

I got up at 3 a.m. and finished off my last book review and commissioned article, and at 9.25 I finished washing up the last of the breakfast things.

At 9.30 the car drew up at the door.

There were four of us—my wife, Gillian, my daughters Lalage, aged fifteen, and Imogen, aged ten. Our baggage consisted of four large suitcases and four small suitcases to be carried in the hand. We also carried a rug, but for once I was adamant about extras. We took no packets of sandwiches or thermos flasks. We were on Oxford platform by 9.40 and there encountered an American lady and her small daughter who was at school with Lalage. The six of us occupied the whole of a carriage to Paddington.

Our conversation was unusual. It consisted solely of reminiscences of the *Yellow Book*. The lady was a niece of Robert Barr and a friend of Bill Nicholson, Orpen, Augustus John, Aubrey Beardsley, and Sargent. It was, I felt, an auspicious start.

On our arrival at Paddington we joined the usual long and ultra-patient queue for taxis and I despatched my family with the hand-baggage to the Milestone Hotel, Kensington Court, while I took a second taxi to Victoria with the heavy luggage to be registered. My driver was Dickensian in his geniality, another happy omen. He told me that he was seventy-seven. The porter at Victoria was bent, pallid, and crabbed. His age was sixty-two. He looked like Rip Van Winkle. He explained the discrepancy by accusing the taxi-driver of leading a gentleman's life, working when he pleased, and described his own as being a slave's existence.

"In the last war I came 'ome from Ypres and got to Victoria beat to the wide. There was a taxi-driver there. It was four in the morning. 'E asked five bloody quid to drive me to the Old Kent Road. I said I'd see 'im in 'ell first, and I walked it with my 90lb. pack on my back. I've never forgotten."

I registered my luggage. It came to 110lb. and I was charged 15s. 6d. for it. I then drove to Manetta's for a farewell luncheon with the publisher of this book, an elder daughter who was going out to the South of France the following day, and my family.

Manetta's is expensive but it is good value. The service is excellent, the food appetising, and the drink not prohibitive. I paid 20s. for a bottle of Constanza, a sweet woman's drink, by which I mean that it is both sweet and meet for a sweet woman.

I then took the family by way of the Swiss Federal Railway office where I got my *abonnement* to the Haymarket Gaumont to see a film adapted from Graham Greene's novel *The Man Within*. The adaptation was a wholly unworthy and grotesque travesty of a remarkable novel. To secure a happy ending complete nonsense had been made of the plot. To satisfy the delicacy of filmgoers the relations between the hero and the light o' love Lucy were entirely altered and so the whole story became meaningless.

I came out profoundly angry and dissatisfied. I then whisked the family off to a flat in Kensington Gore where we sat on a bed and had a foretaste of our Continental journey listening to a group of Jugo-Slavs and Turks talking volubly in their respective tongues. I learnt that the Slavs approve of the architecture of Oxford. The men of the party gave their vote in favour of polygamy and the women in favour of polyandry, so we all dispersed in harmony.

Six of us dined at the Normandie wisely and well for £3 17s. 6d. and by 9.30 we were all safely in bed at the Milestone Hotel.

Succeeding a high gale came quiet.

Thursday 10th April was the first cloudless day for four months. I got up and looked out of the window over Kensington Gardens and the Serpentine. The sky was blue, the air warm, but the trees were quite bare of buds. Spring had never been more backward.

We had an adequate breakfast, but the bill for the four of us, £4 5s. 6d. for bed and breakfast, struck me as high. We had to wait for so long for a taxi that we started to walk with our bags to catch a bus.

I deposited the hand-baggage at Victoria and we then drove to Bumpus's—where Mr Wilson immediately took me into his office and cajoled me into writing a brief summary of twenty lectures on the whole course of English Literature.

I sat in my shirt-sleeves in the sun surrounded by tins of snuff and cups of tea and set to work after despatching my family to see a sick school-friend of Lalage's.

I finished my superhuman effort at 11.30, after one of the most concentrated hours of work in my life.

I was interrupted by Lady Birkett to whom I read an extract of Peattie's work, an American bacteriologist of extraordinary breadth of vision. My family returned. I bought a *Macbeth* to read with Lalage, a *Traveller's Log Book* for Imogen who was as usual entranced, Christine Stead's novel *Letty Fox* (15s. for a novel!) for my wife, and *Brighter French* for myself.

Armed for the journey we drove to Victoria and lunched very adequately if slowly at the station Continental Restaurant. It was as usual very full. We got away by one o'clock and went down to join the queue at the barrier of No. 7 platform.

The crowd was uninspiring. It was being shepherded by uniformed guides wearing the cap and badge of Lunn, Frame, Cook and Polytechnic. We spent our time of waiting looking for possible spies. They all looked so ordinary that they might all have been spies.

At 1.30 we were allowed on to the platform, and Lunn's man showed us to our reserved seats. I then went off to the Customs to see the registered baggage put through. The Customs officer was a young sailor who, reading the label on my suitcase, said, " Off in search of more material?"

I agreed.

" I hope you're more accurate than last time," he said. " You went wrong once or twice over Scotland."

I told him that I would remember his warning and returned to my carriage.

Precisely at 1.50 the Boat Express drew out.

Our companions were two pleasant-looking young girls who told me that they too were going to Montreux. Their home town was Cambridge and neither of them had ever been out of England before. I applauded their decision to leave a too drab, restricted England and wondered what lay in store for these innocents abroad.

My elder daughter explained with some detail the products and staple industries of Kent and surprised me by knowing through which towns the Darent and Medway ran. They obviously teach geography thoroughly at Cheltenham.

We then had an instructive game guessing which five out of a mixed bag of ten photographs depicted in the *Daily Express* were murderers.

" 'Tis a pity there's no art," quoted Lalage, " to find the mind's construction in the face."

I looked out of the window on the naked hop-poles of Paddock Wood. It was a perfect English spring day, but the land after its long winter lay arid and bare.

"There," I pointed, "are the North Downs. The Pilgrims' Way."

It was kind of Lalage to refrain from reminding me that she knew the Kentish landscape from her geography lessons. I could tell from the look in her eyes that she did.

We arrived at Folkestone and our first sight of the sea, the surface of which was unruffled.

" We're in luck," I said.

We queued to show our passports. We went off to claim our baggage. A dark-eyed smiling officer read the label on my bag.

" Off in search of more material?"

I agreed, and to forestall his next statement told him that I would try to be accurate.

We climbed the gangway of s.s. *Canterbury* and after seizing deck-chairs and depositing our bags on them on the starboard side (why is that the better side?) joined the queue down below for tea. It was already a long queue and we failed to get into the first-class cabin. We went for a long crocodile round the lower deck and were rewarded by fried eggs and a thin rasher of excellent bacon for which we paid 4s. 6d. each.

At 4.50 we left our moorings and smoothly set out for the already visible white cliffs of Calais. I pointed out the great castle of Dover and the Pharos to my children who were watching puffins, gannets, and porpoises who were following in our wake.

" Why is it called a wake?" asked Imogen. I didn't of course know. I took her for a walk round the ship. I took a photograph of the family group. We watched a large liner coming up Channel.

" From America to Hamburg," I said.

Luckily Imogen refrained from saying, " How do you know?"

Two North Country women burst into song. I didn't blame them. I too felt like singing. I was free of the land of deprivations and don'ts.

" Are we halfway yet?" asked Imogen when we had covered about two hundred yards.

" Don't be silly," said Lalage.

" I'm not being silly," said Imogen. " Are we halfway yet?"

I had never seen the English Channel in this mood. I looked back without regret to my native shores. I felt that I should not care if I never saw them again. England had turned sour on us. I wanted to forget. I looked out on the clear untroubled waters over which flew the gulls, into which dived the gannets and through which the porpoises rolled.

" I wish we were going to America," I said.

" That's not your usual comment," said my wife.

Imogen and I went in search of the bar.

" Can I come in?" she asked.

" We have left the land of Eternal Noes," I said. " You can do anything you like." She did.

I drank a lot of gin. She drank a little orangeade.

At 6.30 we backed into Calais harbour and were standing wedged in a mighty phalanx of our fellow men when Imogen asked me another awkward question.

" I said that you could do what you liked, where you liked. Here is the time and place."

After a little demur she agreed.

The ship was tied up. We descended the gangway.

"Welcome to France," I said and we went to have our pass-ports examined and declare our money. I had one pocket-book (the gift of Lalage) full of tickets, another pocket-book (the gift of Lalage) full of Swiss money and travellers' cheques, and a third pocket-book (the gift of Lalage) filled with eighty one-pound notes.

We were shown into our seats by Lunn's man, and having put down our baggage climbed into the dining-car and began to drink and nibble bread. We had a bottle of Geisweiler and a bottle of Evian. Then, as time was hanging on our hands, I went in search of the bookstall and bought a French illustrated paper full of pictures of naked women and a copy of *The Times* for 4½d.

I discovered that the French franc was worth a halfpenny and the Swiss franc 1s. 2d. Easy to remember.

Our dinner for four plus service charge came to 355.80 frs. and our drinks (two vermouths, one wine, half-litre claret, two Benedictines) to 59 frs.

We were supposed to leave Calais at seven o'clock. We sat looking out on drab sheds till eight o'clock. The sun had set and there was little to see beyond rubble. The war had not dealt kindly with Calais. The houses were roofless; the harbour had been heavily bombed.

Armed with an apple pasty (*chausson aux pommes*) that she couldn't eat, Imogen led the way past an unending line of passen-gers lined up for the second, third, fourth, and fifth dinners to our carriage where we found a red-faced farmer with his wife and two daughters in possession of the remaining four seats.

He told me that he was a fruit farmer at Cottenham near Cambridge and had been flooded out. He was en route for Lugano.

Imogen began throwing a new Sorbo ball about and lost it under the seat.

I read Ann Petry's novel *The Street*, a most moving story of a lovely negress in New York who strove to keep her eight-year-old son and herself above water without sleeping with men. She failed and was driven to murder.

I was very much moved by it. It struck me as plausible. The agony of the fight against poverty has seldom been portrayed with more vigour or accuracy.

As night fell we put out the lights and the eight of us sought in vain for sleep. We stopped at Rheims and at Laon. We had to guess that it was Rheims, but Laon's name was prominently displayed at least a dozen times on the platform.

We lolled, we sat up, we sat back. Our legs got in the way of other legs. We all looked and were extremely uncomfortable. Somebody was lucky enough to snore. We did not look attractive. At four o'clock I went for a walk. The passengers in the other compartments looked even less attractive, except for one honeymoon couple who made no pretence of sleeping. They were very much awake and aware of the presence of each other.

At four o'clock I decided to shave before the queue began.

The first lavatory I tried possessed no mirror. The second possessed no light, but on the ledge I discovered a drab purse containing a one-pound note and some loose silver. It also contained a slip announcing that the owner, a servant of the Ministry of Health, was in receipt of a monthly income of £13 5s. 6d. It seemed inadequate for a Continental traveller. I pocketed the purse and later handed it to Lunn's man who found the owner.

In my search for the switch I pulled (luckily without any evil consequences) the communication cord.

The third lavatory contained no water and the fourth had one tap marked CHAUD which was falsely named. It emitted a tiny trickle of ice-cold water in which I shaved and felt in consequence much fresher.

At 5.45 the birds began to sing and the dawn broke. It was again a cloudless day.

The land was no longer flat. It had become an undulating country of straight hedgeless roads, mixed pasture and arable, with many poplars and silver birches. The farms were all red-roofed. There were no animals out in the fields. Presumably they were still indoors to judge from the manure heaps which were piled high near the tall wood piles. I was struck by the neatness and cleanliness everywhere, especially of the innumerable wayside stations. All the houses possessed green shutters and the majority of these shutters were closed.

At 6.30 we passed Versone and I saw my first tree of almond blossom sweetening the air and colouring the landscape.

There was rime on the grass.

My Cambridgeshire farmer woke up. In answer to all my queries he said, "That's quite right." I felt that I should have liked him as my examiner at Oxford.

Forests covered the distant hills, obviously the Vosges, where my elder daughter had suffered unpleasant things at the hands of the Germans in a concentration camp.

The Cambridgeshire farmer called my attention to woods carpeted with white violets. My wife who knows a lot about wild flowers woke up to disagree violently. "They're anemones," she said and went to sleep again before the farmer could say, "That's quite right." The farmer then saw cherry trees. He saw nothing but cherry trees from then on and said so, often. I was watching the peasants yoking the fat oxen to the plough, sometimes two bullocks, sometimes a bullock and a horse, sometimes one ox. It was all very peaceful, but I missed the presence of sheep and the sight of birds on the wing.

Lalage woke to become geographical.

"That," she said, "is the Schwarzwald. The valley of the Rhine. The Danube rises in the Vosges."

I was not prepared to query it.

"That's quite right," I said.

The farmer's disease was catching.

Imogen's first intimation of the approach of Basle was a glimpse of its Zoo. From that moment she became pure Swiss.

We arrived at Basle exactly an hour late, at 9 a.m. on Friday 11th April.

I set foot on Swiss soil for the first time for twenty-five years.

Again we joined a long and slow-moving queue, first to have our passports examined, then to claim our meal tickets. We then dashed, bags in hand, in search of breakfast. I have vivid memories of breakfasts in that vast station refreshment room. An extraordinarily good-looking Swiss waiter brought a dozen rolls, a plate filled with pats of butter, large jugs of coffee and hot milk, and we settled down to two eggs apiece and bacon, followed by cherry jam, such cherry jam as only the Swiss can make. The bill came to 19 frs.—£1 2s. 6d.

"It's real butter," said Imogen.

"It's white bread," said Imogen.

"They're real eggs," said Imogen.

She is already well on the way to becoming a gourmet.

Breakfast over, I went downstairs to wash, and catastrophe overtook me. I left my fifteen-shilling novel, Christine Stead's *Letty Fox* which I had bought in Bumpus's the day before, on the shelf. I found the family waiting for me at the station entrance impatient for the shops.

"Mummy," said Imogen, "has seen some monkey-nuts."

"That's nothing," I said. "I've seen cigars and cherry brandy. We'll get them when we come back."

Lalage was surveying the wide street.

"How clean everything is," she said.

We stood still and marvelled.

"No smoke," said Imogen.

We asked our way to the shops and everybody said, "Please."

We walked down an avenue with trees in full bud and beds of daffodils dancing before our eyes. Some men were planting shrubs of azaleas. At the bottom of the avenue we turned left.

"All the traffic's going on the wrong side of the road," said Imogen.

"Or are we wrong?" I asked.

I was fast losing my sense of patriotism. We began to pass and then not to pass the shops.

The first stopping-place was a stocking shop.

"Not nylons, please," said Lalage.

We compromised on two pairs for 17s. (not nylons).

Our second stopping-place was a pencil shop. We emerged the richer by two six-coloured pencils and the poorer by £1 5s.

"Not for me," said Lalage, "they're a waste of money."

Our third stopping-place was for me.

"A pair of field-glasses—*vite*," I said, "I've a train to catch."

"Magnificent," said the shopkeeper leading me by the arm into the street. I looked through the glasses. I saw nothing.

"Magnificent," I said. "*Combien?*"

"A hundred and ninety francs," he replied.

"I'll take them," I said and translated the sum as £10 1s.

The last pair I bought cost me sixteen guineas.

My wife at first thought they were a bad buy because they had no case.

"You can't look through a case," I said.

Lalage went white as a sheet.

"You'll soon have no money left," she said.

"That's quite right," I said.

I entered a watch shop.

There was a steel-cased wrist-watch. It contained every gadget that I most want, a luminous dial, the day of the week and month, the phases of the moon, and I think a sliderule and logarithmic tables.

"*Combien?*" I asked.

The girl said, "Three hundred and ninety francs." I translated that as £23.

I hadn't as much in Swiss francs on me. I had started the day with 640 francs. I seemed to have reduced that to a few five-franc notes.

"It's fantastic," said Lalage.

"That's quite right," I said. "It's time to go."

We went, Lalage jubilant, I as sad as Adam leaving the Garden of Eden.

We regained the station at 11.20. We picked up the baggage and joined a queue composed mainly of underfed tiny little gnome-like children, refugees obviously, and when we reached our train found a Travel Agency courier (not Lunn's) trying to bar our way to the through coach to Montreux.

I deposited my bags and family and went back with Imogen to buy a bottle of fizzy orangeade which fizzed all over the platform, three Havana cigars in gold bands at a franc apiece, a flask of cherry brandy at 4s. 6d. and three huge bags of monkey-nuts at a price that I failed to calculate. On my return I found Lalage so white with fury at my extravagance that she refused to accept a bag of monkey-nuts in spite of my lying assurance that they cost a penny a packet.

At 11.46 our journey through Switzerland began.

In our carriage were the two girls from Cambridge and two elderly colourless women who had brought their own sandwiches. All the eight of us immediately broke into transports of delight as we looked out on the colourful and clean wooden chalets that lined our route like spectators clustering to watch a royal train go by.

There were yellow feathery weeping willows. There was a shop window gay with roses, white lilac and sweet-peas.

We went for a very long walk to join the luncheon car. It was filled with business men smoking Havana cigars at a franc a time. I had the good fortune to sit near a most attractive young girl with black hair that fell loosely on her shoulders, slim legs made slimmer by nylon stockings, a straight small nose, a smiling mouth, black liquid eyes, small hands, and a tiny waist. I felt envious of her companion and thought how much more attractive she would have found my conversation.

Then I looked at my own family and was content.

We ate mushrooms on toast, fish with spinach and green salad, followed by dessert, a banana, an apple, and an orange, which sent Imogen into an ecstasy of delight.

I heard church bells ringing melodiously and said so. Lalage reminded me with some asperity that they were cow-bells.

"That's quite right," I said.

A river ran below.

"The Aar," said Lalage.

"That's quite right," I said.

There were steep grassy slopes on the left of the train leading up to wooded knolls. There was no gap between villages. I felt that most of Switzerland's four million inhabitants must live in Basle or Berne or on the main road that connects them. There was, I remember, a place called Zurich. I noticed (aloud) that all the chalet roofs were unusually steep.

"So that the snow can fall off them easily," said Lalage.

"That's quite right," I said

Then I suddenly forgot the appeal of the green shutters and the blue of the peasants' boiler-suits.

I had seen the vision, the spotless sunkissed white of distant peaks. I became on that instant transfigured.

"Snow," said Lalage.

"That's quite right."

I felt that after long absence I had come home. I had never felt like this about Switzerland in the past. I had no warning that I was going to feel like this about it now. It was quite uncanny. Just a turn of the screw, a sight of white peaks in the far distance, and I felt my burden fall. I was within sight of home. This was where I belonged. My spirit was in the Alps.

Vaguely I noticed a superb medieval castle, bedding hung out of the chalet windows in the sun, the sound of birds singing, the sight of more and more blossom.

My mind was on the hills.

We drew into Berne.

The dining-car stopped there so we walked down the platform to regain our compartment and as we drew near we saw the train begin to move. Imogen leapt aboard, so did my wife, so did I, so did not Lalage.

I looked out on the receding platform and the figure of my forlorn and startled daughter alone and looking as if she were seeing us off for the last time.

The other occupants of our carriage were sympathetic and dismayed.

"You take it very calmly," they said.

"That's quite right," I replied.

We stopped. We backed into another platform. There was the smiling Lalage.

"You never gave me any money," she said, "so I decided to walk."

"Quite right," I said. "It's less than a hundred miles."

The train again got under way. We raced over ravines, past thundering waterfalls, through dense forests. These things mattered not at all. I hardly noticed them. I was too excited. We were getting nearer and nearer to the snowclad peaks.

Great craggy peaks pointed to the sky.

"They're like the Cuillin," said my wife.

"That's quite right," I said. "Perhaps a little higher."

"Hannibal must have had quite a job crossing them," said Imogen.

"That's quite right," I said.

We came to Fribourg with its romantic castle walls and imposing church tower. We stopped at a wayside station and a lizard on the opposite platform obligingly went through its repertoire to amuse Imogen. She was about to leave the train to coax it into her lap when we moved on.

I gazed through my glasses at the slopes of the Eiger, Mönch, and the Jungfrau.

I was wrong about those glasses. The man had been right. They were magnificent. I could see the slopes down which I had skied twenty-five years before. They defied description. I saw a man on horseback, boys putting a mattress out on the roof.

"The Swiss love to lie in the sun," said one of the colourless women.

"That's quite right," I said.

I watched a kestrel hover.

My mind was concentrated on the Alps.

There were red-roofed houses standing bare in midfield, gentle slopes leading up to thick woods, hedgeless roads going on and on. We came to Romont with its high needle-point of a spire and round tall prehistoric dun.

I saw my first sheep. They were black.

But my mind was concentrated on the eternal white of the snow.

An informative ticket-collector pointed.

"Dent du Midi—Mont Blanc——"

I gazed at the tremendous peaks holding up the sky.

We passed into a tunnel, a long one. We emerged into a different world, a world of vineyards occupying the whole of a hillside.

"It faces south," said Lalage.

"That's quite right," I said.

"Look—look, oh look," said Imogen.

I looked.

Far below lay the waters of a vast sea, blue as the Mediterranean and quite unruffled.

"The Lake of Geneva," said Lalage.

"That's quite right," I said.

The hillside was dotted with exquisite villas.

"I'd like to stay here for ever," said Lalage.

We raced along the top of the hillside, curving in and out, and at 3.15 pulled in to Lausanne. It seemed full of exciting hotels. We waited half an hour and were then hooked on to another train.

We discovered an observation-car.

We started again and ran alongside and only a little above the rocky beach.

"There are diving-boards," said Imogen.

"That's quite right," I said.

"If you say that once more," said my wife, "I shall scream and then leave the train."

"I won't," I said, and didn't.

I watched a sailing-boat and some men rowing. I looked across the lake at the French Alps rising sheer out of the water. Cow-bells were ringing.

We stopped at a number of little stations. Eventually we arrived at Montreux. Twenty-seven hours had passed since we left Victoria. We were met by an affable Lunn's man. We climbed into a taxi, drove through streets crowded with hotels to Territet, and pulled up at the Hotel Bonivard, a white hotel overlooking the lake on the mountain side, above the Castle of Chillon. We were shown our rooms, high up facing the lake.

We descended to tea on the terrace. There was cherry jam.

We boarded a tram. " Buy a season," said the hotelier.

We got off in the town centre.

We bought 500 grams of mixed chocolates (no coupons) for 6s. 6d., six picture postcards each, a sponge for £1, a book on Switzerland for £1, a map for 1 fr. 75 c., and a silver snuff-box for 8s.

The shops were wonderful.

I sat on a seat on the front listening to the lapping of the waves and looking at the snow-clad hills. The sun glistened on the still lake. Lovely girls moved slowly past. Life was perfect. The birds sang their evensong. A raven floated above the peaks. I gazed at him through my glasses. Everybody seemed happy and carefree. The Swiss had endured no war.

I was at home. As I watched the tops of the peaks change to rose-pink in the setting of the sun my happiness was complete.

We took a tram back to dinner as the sun set behind Geneva. There were three jolly-looking young English girls who got off at the Bonivard and ran up the hill.

At 7.30 we dined. The visitors in the main seemed lifeless and old. We drank Asti. Lalage, dropping with sleep, went to bed.

I too went upstairs and gazed out over the still lake and watched the ring of twinkling lights.

The Alps had disappeared into the night.

I went to bed.

Saturday, 12th April, 1947

AT dawn the birds gradually began their crescendo of praise. They began at 5.15. I got up to see why their note was so full of joy. The sight that met my eyes took me straight back to Homer. Rosy-fingered was his phrase, and rosy-fingered is right.

At the setting of the sun last night I had seen the white snow change subtly to rose-pink and at the sun-rising again the snow was rose-pink above the blackness of the massifs that had not yet blushed to receive their morning kiss.

As I lay in bed listening to the lapping of the waves on the rocky shore far below I became conscious of certain outstanding features about the Swiss people and their land that I had overlooked in my first day's excitement. The most noticeable fact about the people is their unfussiness. They go about their business quietly and competently like their electric trains. They hold themselves well, they are neat and colourful without gaudiness, the men are well built and good-looking, the women inspire confidence and respect. They are invariably ready to help the foreigner and their friendliness is warm without being effusive. I have no statistics on the subject but I am prepared to bet that their percentage of suicides is lower than ours. There is a noticeable absence of worry here and plenty of evidence of wealth.

They have enough elbow-room not to get in each other's way. Their chalets in the country and their villas in the towns are splendidly spaced. I have yet to see any trace whatever of a slum.

Switzerland may not be Utopia, but it is quite easily the nearest approach to Utopia that I have yet seen.

The people live comfortably in surroundings that are quite impossible to describe. I have never seen more luxurious cars than I have in the main street of Montreux. I have never seen shops display such a lavish variety of luxury goods. I have never seen houses of greater magnificence. The efficiency of the people may be judged from their engineering. The Alps have proved an insurmountable obstacle to every enemy, yet they have had to yield their proud secret to their native architects. There is no such thing as the back of beyond. Even the most remote Alpine valley has been turned into a highway with fertile fields and an electric railway. The bridges, viaducts and tunnels are a revelation not only of the engineer's genius but also of the native good taste.

It is certainly true that in winter the beasts live under the same roof as their masters, but both beast and man preserve a cleanliness that must make the Swiss regard the English as Yahoos.

Perhaps the predominating quality of the country after its beauty is its quietude. At any time of day, even in a town like Montreux, the main sounds are those of water lapping, bells ringing and birds singing.

On this second day I got up early to sit at my bedroom window and looked out across the water at the snowy crags change colour as the sun rose over the back of the eastern hills.

It was with some difficulty that I got my family down to breakfast by nine o'clock. The air had taken instant effect.

After our chocolate, rolls and marmalade we set out for the ski slopes above Gstaad. On boarding the tram I bought a season ticket for the whole family for two francs. A season ticket is an immense saving, because the day before it had cost me well over two francs to take the family into and out of Montreux once.

This *abonnement* is a rectangular yellow ticket covered with figures. I discovered with some difficulty that it was valid for nearly three years and for forty-five journeys of five centimes.

My first call in Montreux was the very imposing Banque Populaire where I handed over a wad of travellers' cheques and the accompanying authorisation forms to a smiling clerk. He did his best to be helpful but I departed little wiser if somewhat richer for the meeting. He worked out a lot of figures and made me sign a large number of forms after which he decided to allow me 679 frs. 60 c. in cash and 340 frs. in gay pink vouchers, each good for ten francs. Apparently I could draw as many vouchers as I wished but I wasn't allowed to draw more actual cash for ten days.

I found the vouchers complicated.

They were valid only for amounts of five francs and over, and only for the payment of my hotel bill, garage, petrol, railway, boat, official coach and aeroplane journeys.

"The conversion," I read, "of this voucher into cash is not allowed, nor can it be used for shopping purposes."

I wonder what happens if you put one into the collection-box in church. We are so used to restrictions in England that I wasn't bothering overmuch about this voucher game, but I could see at once that it meant going slow on chocolates at 9 frs. per 500 grams (10s. 6d. a pound) and Asti at 10s. a bottle. It meant going on excursions instead of dallying over the counter. Perhaps that is all to the good, but the shops are so inviting that I felt pretty sure I was going to overrun my allowance of petty cash and have to fall back on my reserve of £80.

"It would be a pity to have to do that," said the bank clerk. "We only give 10 frs. 40 c. for one-pound notes."

I felt that England's stock had sunk pretty low.

I am not very clever about money, but at that moment I felt envious of my English friends who had claimed to have come home with more money in their pockets than they had when they set out, after a holiday that had cost them nothing. This was apparently done by the simple expedient of crossing the Italian frontier and selling their one-pound notes for lire at an exorbitant rate and then returning to Switzerland to convert the lire into Swiss francs and so back into one-pound notes, or have I got the story wrong?

My sole desire was to convert my vouchers into shopping money and I felt that that ought not to be too difficult. I could scarcely ask the bank clerk to help me to cheat his bank of their right currency, so I went off in search of a post-office.

The bank put all British banks to shame for spaciousness and magnificence, but the post-office was a Palace of Beauty and the official an angel of politeness. He couldn't understand a word I said, but I got what I wanted, forty pink stamps at twenty centimes for postcards, and twenty green stamps at thirty centimes for letters. Time was getting on and I found it difficult to wean my wife from the shop windows. Luckily I had given none of my family any Swiss money at all.

We arrived at the station, an even more noble and spacious building than the bank and the post-office, and found that tickets were obtainable on the platform from which we were to leave. This was an occasion for vouchers. I decided to travel second-class. It was only after I had seen the price on the ticket to Gstaad, 23 frs. 50 c. for each of us return, that I felt that I ought to have gone third.

Later I decided that I had been right, not because of the luxurious cushions provided in the second-class compartment which we had to ourselves, but because of the window-space. It was a journey up and through the mountains that demanded constant running from one side of the carriage to the other to catch a glimpse of some ever fresh magnificence.

The platform was crowded with skiers, most of them bronzed, all of them lithe and fit.

A train came in bound for Milan.

A batch of English schoolgirls, fat and frowsty and far less prepossessing than the Swiss children, gesticulated and fussed as they ran like sheep being herded to market.

A lean tanned skier passed wearing a topi, then two Chinese men and a group of Egyptians. A blue-smocked porter staggered along under a load of silver cow-bells, and another followed with a trolley-load of gay flowers in pots.

The Swiss are very flower-minded.

At 10.45 we moved out and began our steep curving climb in and out among the vineyards and villas above Montreux. We kept on looking down on the town and lake now from one side, now from the other. I noticed a number of beehives, all painted red and white and green. I saw a group of cypress trees towering above a churchyard. Then as we climbed further up we came to a vast medieval château with battlements set on a rock and a plateau overlooking the lake. Then came a huge sanatorium and a succession of steep fields that were carpeted with cowslips and wild crocuses. The cowslips were the first that I had seen this year.

Each year we have a competition in the family, and the one who sees the first cowslip, sees the first swallow, or hears the first cuckoo gets five shillings.

"Five shillings for the first bear," I shouted.

"Are there really bears in Switzerland?" asked Imogen.

"There are," I said.

We were above the level of the houses and Imogen began to feel the height. We were now completely away from the town, but there was no sign of cattle in the fields.

"They keep them in late," said Jill.

"Not enough grass," I said. "Look at it."

It was indeed as short and smooth and close-cropped as the grass on our South Downs.

We began to run through a pine forest, over narrow viaducts above deep ravines with falling cataracts. Everywhere there were field-paths.

We came to Les Avants where boys and girls were playing tennis in front of a large school called Châtelard. There were

children on roller skates, and children carrying skis. It seemed to
be a colony of children.

I looked up to a peak where the sun shone on the crisp virgin
snow and made it look like a gigantic knight in burnished white
armour.

We entered a long tunnel and emerged at Les Casses where
our ski-runners left us. We were on the snow line and about to
run down the sides of a ravine into a distant valley. A high black
crag towered above us on the opposite side of the ravine, but the
valley was cultivated the whole way down and there was a
station almost every mile. The slopes were covered with wild
flowers of every sort, the crocus and cowslip predominating. At
Allières we came into the land of timber yards and at Les Sciernes
the little hedges had been neatly trimmed.

So we wound and twisted our way to the foot of the valley
to reach Montbovon where we joined the main line from Berne
to Thun and made a sharp right-hand turn up another valley
and followed the course of a river with crystal clear green water.
The whole valley was dotted with small wooden chalets with
roof slats steeply set made of dove-grey wood.

At La Tire we came to a land that was still green but the
slopes were perfect for skiing.

At Rossinière we passed a little white gem of a church and
looked up at a fresh succession of Alpine peaks with vast woods
on their lower slopes. The fields on either side of the river were
being manured. The valley widened and the number of chalets
increased rapidly as we drew nearer to Château d'Oex.

I have always wanted to visit this famous skiing centre. In
midwinter it becomes a seething mass of riotous holiday-makers.
It now lay quiet and lovely under the hot spring sun.

I first noticed the red-roofed church on a knoll, then a second
church, then its hotels, main shopping streets and hundreds of
little wooden chalets with protruding eaves dotted along the
gentle slopes. It struck me as ideal for the beginner because of the
number of nursery slopes.

I could not see where the more adventurous skiers got their
runs, because the high Alps lay well back with thick woods at
their feet. Then came the hamlet of Les Granges with well
scrubbed tables shining in the sun.

The colour of the rock changed from dead white to pink

granite. The wonderful smooth road ran alongside the railway and the river ran alongside the road. One stupendous bare crag dominated the western side of the valley which was much more populated than I expected. Men were felling and stripping timber, other men were muck-spreading, women and children were bending over cultivated patches hoeing.

Then we came to Rougemont with its octagonal shingled church spire and vast white clock with gold hands. Here we saw a group of well fed Jersey cattle being taken out for the first time after the long winter.

We passed a deserted airfield at Saanen where I saw a field of anemones, and so we came to the head of the valley at Gstaad, to which place I had sent my skis twenty-five years before and had never found time to reclaim them.

We were met by my smiling host, who, to the almost uncontrollable delight of Imogen, led us to an open drosky or horse-carriage in which we drove in state through the village street, under the vast Palace Hotel and so on up through the woods by the side of a rushing stream to the ski-hoist.

He gave Imogen no time to think but took her on his knee into the chair, and I stepped into the neighbouring one and in my excitement forgot to bar myself in.

We set off across the ravine to climb the Wasserngrat. I found it quite terrifying for the first five seconds. Imogen clutched my hand in hers tight and bit her lips. Our host blithely pointed out peaks that I daren't look at.

"Don't look down," I said to Imogen. "Look up."

The wheels creaked over the cable. We crawled up very slowly. The grass beneath was never more than twenty feet below but the slope was considerable.

There was, I knew, nothing to fear in the hands of the capable Swiss, but my ears began to sing. I clutched my maps and note-book more and more tightly and gave an occasional quick glance at the surrounding peaks.

Gstaad is three thousand five hundred feet above sea level. When we had been hoisted two thousand feet we came to a shed exactly at the foot of the snow line. We disembarked only to re-embark immediately in a second hoist which carried us over the snow slopes that were infinitely steeper to the top of the Wasserngrat, eight thousand feet above sea level.

I have seldom been more relieved to leave a vehicle. I prefer droskies. But now that I was on land again I looked round. I was right on top of the world completely encircled by peak after peak, range upon range of Alps.

Northward I looked down the steep slopes to the quiet and lovely village of Gstaad with its vast white Palace Hotel standing high up in the centre. My host pointed out a nearby chalet. "That's where Montgomery spent last winter," he said. "We liked him. He gave us a cup for the ski jump. We get more sun here than any other place in the Bernese Oberland."

"Say the world," I said as I looked on the sun-kissed earth.

"Nine hours is our average," he said. "You see it lies open in a wide valley and all the hills lie back." He pointed to ski-hoists ascending other peaks.

"The last time I skied," I said, "I had to climb in skis."

"Those days are over," he said. "The joy in skiing lies in rushing down, not in crawling up."

My eye fell on groups of men and women wearing sunglasses and very little else lying on mattresses outside the chalet.

It also fell on others sitting at the tables outside the chalet having lunch.

"I expect you're feeling hungry," said our host.

There seemed no point in denying it.

The Alpine air induces sleep. It also induces a thirst and an appetite.

I couldn't take in the scene at all.

Here I was eight thousand feet above sea level, whisked up without any effort on my part, about to sunbathe, about to eat and drink. The first thing I did was to take off my overcoat, three waistcoats and most of the rest of the clothes that would be essential for an English April day.

I then began looking through my glasses. The scene was still far too vast for me to comprehend.

I was standing sizzling in the sun half-naked. Skiers were flashing past me, christying down slopes of a terrifying angle; sunbathers with skins the colour of old parchment were basking with closed eyes; my host's small son was playing with a spaniel called Scarletti round a snowman who showed signs of melting; waiters were walking round with drinks; I was eight thousand feet up, the sky above me a cloudless blue, the peaks shining white, the valleys a deep green, the forest black. I was drunk with beauty.

" I want to stay up here for ever," said Imogen.

I took out my compass and laid it on the ledge of the balustrade. I took out my map and began to work out a few bearings.

North over Gstaad stood a serried range of fierce black jagged crags, the Cuillin hills immensely magnified. North-east the slopes were gentler but higher and snow-covered. East rose the Mönch, the Eiger and the Jungfrau, my first friends among the Alps. South-east stood the summit of the Wasserngrat.

The chalet stood about two hundred yards below the top to give both protection against the wind and the hardy skiers a little work to do before their descent. It was very steep indeed, and what lay over the top I didn't know.

South lay peak upon peak—Diablerets, the Wildhorn and so on. South-west I recognised the Dent du Midi, the most easily recognisable of all the Alps because of its twin teeth or cat's ears.

Far in the dimness of the west behind a most strange white peak that looked like the end of a chalet with two steep-pitched roofs rose Mont Blanc. North-west over the valley of Gstaad rose the peaks above Montreux.

I was called from my viewing to lunch. I began by throwing a piece of bread into Imogen's too well filled plate of hot soup. The already hot Imogen was now temporarily scalded. I ate a lot of steak, pounds of French beans, and drank enormous quantities of white wine. Then followed pineapple, coffee and kirsch.

In England waiters complain if they have to carry a piece of toast on a tray up one floor. Here I was enjoying a Lucullan feast that had to be hoisted eight thousand feet. More than ever I began to wonder how anybody who could afford it could elect to live anywhere else. Both my hosts, Mr Loozeli and the proprietor of the Palace Hotel who had invited me to lunch, were smiling and obviously extremely happy men. Their wives and families were by their sides enjoying a siesta, and after luncheon both husbands and wives accompanied by the spaniel Scarletti skied down past the chalet to the first hoist halt. I have never seen neater skiing. I watched them from the balcony in silent ecstasy mingled with envy. I wanted Imogen and Lalage to ski as well as that. A bird in flight, a yacht in full sail, an expert skier on a steep and sunny slope are surely the most graceful of all moving things.

I made a sudden determination. Only yesterday I had felt as if I had come home after long years. I worship the sun. My happiness is only complete among the hills.

The skiers returned laughing.

"I can't ski," said my host much in the same way that Shakespeare might have said, "I can't write."

"You're going to teach my Imogen and Lalage."

"I'll be glad," he said.

I turned to the proprietor of the Palace.

"Will you reserve two double rooms facing the sun for me for the Christmas holidays?" I asked.

"I'll be glad," he said.

My heart sang for joy.

I moved away from the people. I lit a cigar. I looked up the slope at the descending skiers. Everyone else wore glasses. I wanted no blinkers. Let the sun blind me if it wished. I was gazing on beauty in her naked blaze.

Then suddenly I caught sight of a black speck soaring high above the summit of the Wasserngrat. Hurriedly I scanned the heavens with my glasses. It was, as I expected, an eagle. The land over which the eagle flies is the land for me.

How many winters I have remaining I do not know. I prayed then to God to make it possible for me to spend them all with my family in Switzerland, at Gstaad in Switzerland.

I felt momentarily sorry for the Swiss who cannot feel the ecstasy that we poor English feel, released from the grey gloom, the damp, the pall of clouds that obscure the sky in the low-lying river valleys, to soar as the eagle soars in the azure empyrean. The change is the change from hell to heaven, and it is truly difficult to think of heaven as more satisfying to the eye and spirit than this.

The Wasserngrat on that Saturday afternoon in April was perfection and I knew it. I had achieved my peak, come what come may.

I wanted time to stand still and the sun to stand still in the heavens.

But God in His mercy permits of no tedious eternity. Time

marches on. We had a train to catch. Even when our host suggested that there were two, I chose the earlier. I dared not risk any diminution of my blessing. I wanted to cut it short abruptly before there was a chance of satiety.

Idly I watched women oiling their legs and backs against the sun. An old woman in a pirate's paper-cap smiled benignly at me as she sat knitting in the sun. I was grateful to her for not saying, "Isn't it wonderful?"

Somebody was telling a girl in a Cambridge blue skiing cap and scarlet tunic about ravens and chamois. "The swallow," he said, "doesn't come till June." How foolish, I thought, of the swallow to come to England in April and leave Switzerland unvisited in the spring.

"And when goes hence?" said I echoing Lady Macbeth.

"In September," said the bird-lover.

"How foolish of the swallow," said I, aloud this time.

Two men came racing down the steep slopes above, taking it nearly straight.

"How like the swallow," I said.

"They're pros," said the Cambridge blue girl with a touch of contempt.

I heard a crash and saw another girl lying on the platform. The Cambridge blue laughed.

"That'll learn her. She only started yesterday. She ought to keep to the nursery slopes."

"She shouldn't try to fly before she can walk," said the bird-lover.

More and more people emerged from the hoist-shed. It was Saturday afternoon. I felt that I wanted to be going. I didn't want to share my Alps. I sought my host inside the chalet, a spotless, neat affair of plain forest fir wood.

He was standing over the picture-postcard box.

"Help yourself," he said.

I helped myself lavishly.

"I think I'll catch the earlier train," I said.

"I'll ski to the halfway hut and come down with you to the station. I'll ring up for the buggy."

"I don't want you to miss this lovely sun," I said.

He looked profoundly shocked.

"I always see my guests off the premises," he said.

At 4.15 Imogen and I no longer hand in hand were swinging pleasantly in mid-air about five thousand feet above Gstaad.

We were now craning our necks and twisting our bodies to look at the skiers flashing past below. Imogen waved.

On the way up neither of us had dared to move a muscle.

How easily we acclimatise ourselves to novelties in Switzerland.

At 4.45 we were sitting in the sun outside the hoist-shed at the foot of the slopes watching lumbermen at work felling the trees across the river. There was no sign of the ordered drosky. My host became restive.

"I'm not bothering," I said. "If we miss it we'll have cherry jam for tea."

"I can promise you that," he said. "But you'll miss the daylight."

"Let's walk," I said.

We sauntered down the narrow track with the music of the burbling streams ringing in our ears.

Halfway down the drosky appeared. The driver was voluble. We drove through the village street, with horse-bells jangling. There seemed to be fascinating shops. One bore the title WOOLLEN GOODS. I visualised Jill at Christmas spending much of her time there.

The train was standing at the platform. It was waiting for the up train to pass.

"Lucky for you," said my host.

"My luck is always in in Switzerland," I said.

I climbed up into the I–II compartment. We had it to ourselves.

The shrill whistle sounded. The train started noiselessly. A ticket-collector appropriated our tickets.

The landmarks looked slightly different on the return journey, but I was able now to formulate a general pattern.

Our way lay along the wide long green valley to Montbovon where it turned sharply left-handed up the ravine which led to the mountain that hid Montreux.

At Allières I noticed a St. Bernard dog harnessed to a "dog-cart" (if that is the name), properly reined. It sat on its haunches, licking its jaws, impatient to be off.

The hewers of wood and spreaders of muck were walking,

pack on back, home after the day's work. They have, I suspect, no half-days on Saturdays in Switzerland, nor dog-racing.

I was fascinated by a long narrow white waterfall. It looked like the long strand of a giant witch's hair.

At Les Casses we were rejoined by a vast army of skiers, one of whom left his sticks behind, and two others missed the train. They didn't fuss. They didn't seem to mind.

We entered the tunnel and emerged at Châtelard School at Les Avants.

We looked down on the lake. Why is it called Lac Léman?

The birds were singing sweetly above Chambéry junction where a crowd of girls joined the train.

We arrived at Montreux at 6.30 to find most of the shops shut.

We decided to book seats for a film *Les Enfants du Paradis*. We were told that children under eighteen were not admitted. How sensible of the Swiss, I thought.

We boarded a tram and handed in our *abonnement* for clipping.

At 7.15 we dined.

The occasion called for another bottle of Asti.

After dinner we found every chair in the lounge occupied.

That did not displease me.

I went to bed.

Sunday, 13th April, 1947

AT 5.15 the birds began to sing, and at 5.30 I watched the procession of cars below going off into the mountains with skis tied behind.

I looked out on to the lake where two pairs of duck were noiselessly diving. I watched the sun tinge the peaks with pink. Another day had begun.

At eight o'clock I breakfasted speedily and without fuss. No waiter dusted the tables. They contained no dust.

There was no English breakfast smell. Everything smelt of flowers. The whole of Switzerland, even to the interior of the trams, smells of flowers. What do the trams that go along the Victoria Embankment smell of? Not flowers, I think.

After breakfast I sat on the hotel terrace in the sun looking down on the gardens, the paths and road that lay below between me and the lake.

Cyclists began to pass on shining aluminium bicycles with packs on their backs. Most of the girls wore thick white woollen stockings which stopped just below the knee. More and more expensive-looking cars purred past almost silently and very quickly. These nearly all had skis strapped along the back, sides and top. Men began to assemble their fishing-rods on the rocks by the shore. Family parties began to form circles on the grass verge by the water and undo picnic baskets.

It was the beginning of Switzerland's weekly break. They have no early closing day. Church bells rang over the water.

My family joined me, and wrote a few postcards. "We mustn't send many," said Lalage, "the postage is too expensive." Then we set off to explore the Castle of Chillon, which stands less than five hundred yards away from the hotel. Lalage led the way down the steep steps and as we crossed the bridge over the railway sternly called our attention to a notice: DANGER DE MORT.

"Don't," she shouted back, "let Imogen pick the flowers."

Imogen immediately explored the railway bank for a posy for our buttonholes. I received a cowslip, a flower of gentian blue, a dandelion and an aconite. Lalage showed her disapproval by walking on ahead along the track that led by the side of the water. Jill stopped to watch an artist who was painting the castle, and Imogen to try to tempt two swans to accept a nosegay. I looked ahead at the castle and thought of Byron.

The exterior of Chillon is smaller than I expected. It is a gem, but a small gem. Appearances are deceptive. The interior is as massive as Carnarvon or Windsor and much more satisfying. Its outside walls are a whitish grey and the roof a deep russet brown. Balconies overlook the water which laps three-quarters of its elliptical shape. One square tower surmounts the rest. To reach it we had to cross a moat and pass through a turnstile.

On payment of the entrance fee which is negligible (1 fr. 80 c. for the four of us on presentation of the *carte de séjour* which reduces the fee by ten per cent) we were presented with a succinct guide-book giving all the practical details of its twenty-four rooms and courtyards and seventeen walls and towers.

We passed over the moat and through the gateway into a

cobbled and sunny courtyard where a group of American soldiers were lavishing many rolls of film on some extremely photogenic American girls.

I found it hard to concentrate on my guide which explained
to me that this fortress built on solid rock " cannot be dated with
any certainty." The girls could be. They were post-war America.
The fortress is primitive. The girls were not. The fortress was
enlarged in the eleventh century, not I was glad to see by the
Normans. I will not pursue the analogy. The fortress was in
those days the property of the Bishop of Sion, then held in fief
by the Counts of Savoy from the twelfth century until 1536,
when it was seized by the Bernese, who held it till 1798. Since
then it has belonged to the Canton of Vaud. A simple history in
keeping with everything Swiss.

It was reached by the ancient road from Italy that ran
over the St. Bernard Pass, and was built to guard the narrow
defile that ran between the lake and the mountains (vast rocks
guard the shore side) and to collect taxes on all passing mer-
chandise.

I walked round and round the cobbled yard looking partly at
the water tower, the loopholes, galleries and exciting fourteenth-
century windows above, and partly at the even more exciting
lovely American girls who chattered and laughed as they were
being photographed at my side.

It is significant that I should have seen practically no Americans at all before this, and that I should meet so many in so
famous an historic shrine. I went below ground to explore a
labyrinth of underground vaults, and passed from a dungeon, in
which still stands a gibbet with its rope that looked well used,
to Bonivard's prison, where an American soldier had posed his
enchanting companion against the third pillar where Byron had
carved his name. I felt that Byron would have written a far
better poem than *The Prisoner of Chillon* had he had the good
fortune to meet, as I was meeting, bevies of such lovely willowy
creatures as were now distracting my attention from the story of
the Prior of Geneva who remained chained for four years to the
fifth pillar in the sixteenth century. The Americans were not interested in the fifth pillar. They concentrated on the Byron
pillar and most appropriately on the sort of thing that most
attracted Byron. We retraced our steps to the first courtyard and

then proceeded by way of a second courtyard to the Grand Hall of the High Bailiff, governor of the Castle. This vast chamber was furnished, as were most of the other rooms, with massive shining refectory tables, chairs and chests. On the floor above we came to the Aula Nova or Festive Hall of the lords of the Castle, the walls of which are festooned with tall pikes and formidable-looking daggers.

Then followed bedrooms with very neat pewter urns and washing basins and so I came to the Coat of Arms Hall, the grand reception hall of the Middle Ages, the walls of which are gay with the colourful escutcheons of the Bernese High Bailiffs of Vevey, lords of the Castle between 1536 and 1733.

Then came the Duke's Chamber, the bedroom of the Counts and Dukes of Savoy with a beautiful ceiling, a room of medieval latrines, the *domus clericorum*, and the chapel which has been restored and is now used for Divine Service.

I passed on into the Grand Hall of the Count, now the Hall of Justice, but in Middle Ages the Lower Grand Hall for banquets. It is remarkable for the beauty of its tall marble pillars and beautiful windows that overlook the lake.

Imogen was more excited by the pillar of the well-room, the torture chamber, and refused to move on until I had given her a lengthy disquisition on the thumbscrew and the stake. Then she fondled the scarred wooden pillar lovingly and said, "Poor prisoners."

In two minutes it was poor Imogen, for we climbed from floor to floor by a succession of narrow wooden ladders with polished banisters to the Keed, or ancient tower of refuge. At the fourth floor her nerve gave way. She who on the previous day had taken to the intimidating ultra-modern ski-hoist was defeated by the ancient steps.

We descended to the fourth courtyard where we saw a massif of solid masonry sloping down to the moat and a long covered patrol gallery. There followed two defence towers and we found ourselves back in the first courtyard, the circle completed, and the American soldiers still standing in the sun, the American girls still posing. It was with great difficulty that I tore myself away and passed out to the flower garden below where stands a noble white marble figure of a kneeling refugee begging for admittance, the work of an Alsatian sculptor presented by

France to Switzerland as a token of gratitude for those who were evacuated during the 1914–18 war.

We then passed on to a kiosk where I bought, despite Lalage's vehement protestations, ten expensive postcards of the Castle and a copy of *The Prisoner of Chillon*.

Armed with this we crossed the road to the lovely Taverne du Château Chillon about which I felt that Villon would have written a fitting ballade, and sat outside in the sun where I drank Campari (which has the reputation of being potent), Jill drank Cinzaud, and Lalage and Imogen sucked two salmon-pink milk-shakes (*frappés*) through a straw.

Three American soldiers lolled against the railings overlooking the water, a wealthy Swiss got out of an immense car and brought his shining blonde consort to the table on one side of us, while four merry Swiss soldiers chattered gaily at the table on the other side.

A steamer passed. The Swiss soldiery rose *en masse* to point their Leicas at it and returned talking English. I drank more and more Campari and thought the world very good.

An Englishman sat alone looking very morose, reading a Sunday paper. I asked him if England stood where England did. He said savagely that the profiteering in the exchange of Swiss, Italian and French francs was being engineered on a gigantic scale by the Jews for the benefit of the Palestine Jews.

"If that's the case," he said, "I'd rather walk home than change a pound note that way."

I could not follow his logic but I applauded his sentiments. A bearded minister in thick black overcoat and black homburg, followed by an enormously fat frau, equally gules, waddled into the restaurant. I read the menu and saw that chicken and châteaubriand steak were both on the card at thirteen and fifteen francs respectively. I had another Campari. The children sucked more milk-shakes. Lalage began to read *The Prisoner of Chillon* aloud.

We all agreed that it was an indifferent poem and on looking at my watch I was staggered to see that it was 1 o'clock.

When we regained the Bonivard our grey-haired fellow countrymen were already rising from lunch.

We helped ourselves lavishly to dishes that escape my memory and at 1.45 we were on the train bound for Montreux.

When we reached the pier we joined a large queue of Cook's and Polytechnic patrons who were waiting for the steamer from Lausanne. I bought return tickets for St. Gingolphe, at 2 frs. 25 c. second-class return.

I listened to a lot of English and basked in the very hot rays of the sun. I began to wish that I had brought a hat.

A distant hoot announced the approach of the steamer, and I watched a sharp-nosed Lilliputian *Queen Elizabeth* cut speedily over the unruffled blue towards us.

Imogen suddenly saw a balloon. With infinite difficulty I fought my way out of the queue and bade her tie her new treasure to a button of her coat.

Imogen is a type of public-school girl of whom I strongly approve. To outgrow one's love of balloons is a sign, to my way of thinking, of degeneracy.

Someone whispered that on the other side of the lake we should pass into France and be able to change ten Swiss francs for one thousand French francs. I thought of the Palestine Jews and wondered if I should be able to withstand the temptation.

The steamer came to her moorings. We struggled to the top deck and elected to sit in the shade and look out from shut windows. It became too hot. We struggled into the open and found even standing-room difficult.

Two elderly men wearing old Etonian ties looked with disfavour on their fellow countrymen. I applauded their point of view and thought how much better to have been born a Swiss until I touched a seated Swiss girl and asked her to move a fraction of an inch to allow my small daughter to sit down. Her male companion, a very young bespectacled student, burst, to my surprise, into a spate of French which even to my understanding was impolite.

My next-door neighbour who was bilingual said to me, "He doesn't like you."

"That's quite right," I said. "Tell him how much I agree."

My companion looked shocked.

"He doesn't like any of us. He doesn't like the British."

"Chuck him overboard," I said. "You're bigger than I am."

My companion turned to the seated Swiss and the altercation then begun became more and more heated.

"I told him that he ought to have gone out to the Front," he said to me during a brief interval in hostilities.

The *non sequitur* seemed to me to be wholly in keeping with our race.

I found an interest more appetising—no, not an American girl, but three buzzards above the trees also in the process of argument. There was, I saw, a nest, and the wife was displaying her attractions to a fellow buzzard who obviously was not the lawful sharer of her nest. Her husband dived out of the blue and threatened the *tertium quid* with violence. That was a passion that I could understand. Birds are in many ways almost human. They too get excited over territorial rights and marital infidelity.

The Alps on the other hand don't care. I lifted up my eyes to the Alps and regained my equanimity.

We put in at the pier at Territet and were joined by a group of giggling gawky schoolgirls, unmistakably English. We put in at Villeneuve, Montreux-Plage.

We skirted the eastern shore, which was covered with low feathery trees. Here Lalage became geographical.

"That," she said, "is the mouth of the Rhône."

I was disappointed by its lack of breadth. We called at Borboret and disembarked at St. Gingolphe, for Switzerland a quite untidy place. We climbed a hill and turned right-handed to cross a small bridge guarded by gendarmes. I produced my passport, and while the gendarme turned the pages over this way and that uncertainly I wondered whether or not I should succumb to the temptation to change many francs. I was saved from moral degradation by the gendarme who pushed me rather rudely back. "To Lausanne," he said, "for a visa." I suddenly felt that I didn't want to visit France.

I looked over the bridge at the tiny stream that separated the two countries and thought of the stream of French refugees who must have crossed that water to seek sanctuary from the Germans. I thought too of the innumerable spies who must have got across just here.

I went back to the main street in search of sun and a drink. I was startled to find myself the object of voluble abuse from another young Swiss to whose head the drink had certainly gone.

"He feels, I take it, no great affection for the British," said one of the elderly old Etonians who was by my side.

"Patriotism," I said, "must have some outlet."

St. Gingolphe, I decided, had no great attraction for me. I went back to the boat, and sat in the sun.

To my delight the hooter went and we set sail at least half an hour before the advertised time, leaving by far the greater bulk of our fellow passengers marooned.

I ordered tea and received coffee and rolls. When the time came to pay the waiter demanded meal tickets. "It's to save buying butter on the black market," he said.

It sounded like something out of the Mad Hatter's tea party. I couldn't see the connection.

I didn't really care. I was too happy just sitting in the sun.

The return journey flashed past all too quickly. I saw a girl in white rowing in a green boat with vividly scarlet oars. I watched two amorous kestrels. I watched two not less amorous Americans and thought how wise they were to bring their own women with them.

I tried to find the ticket-collector and Imogen tried to find the *salle des dames*.

We picked up more and more sunburnt returning voyagers. At six o'clock we disembarked at Montreux and joined the immense throng that packed the promenade.

We resisted the temptation to try the swingboats at the fair. We fell to the temptation to join the drinkers in a pension garden. As they had neither Campari nor milk-shakes we left the dim tea-drinkers and boarded a tram for Chillon, not to visit the Castle but the Taverne.

Once more we sat in the sun drinking Campari and sucking milk-shakes through a straw and felt that we had come home again.

We sat back, idly watching the passing procession of cars containing exhausted skiers, of aluminium bicycles pedalled by white-stockinged girls, the heavier by freights of multi-coloured flowers. A sinister Swiss in black to whose head either the sun or the Campari had gone cried to me, "H'lo, old boy."

He resented, I think, my red shirt. I found it more comfortable to sit in my shirt-sleeves.

At seven o'clock we returned to the hotel by way of a path that was haunted with lizards.

The others went up to wash.

49

There was an extremely attractive girl with glistening dark hair that fell over her shoulders, sitting on the edge of a chair, dangling a very shapely leg.

There was one other man in the room, younger than myself, but not much.

She chose him.

"I've lost my train," she said.

Her voice was that of Circe, slow and languorous.

"You've made a very short stay," came the reply.

"I've come to the end of my money," she said. "I've got to go home. Besides, I work."

"Can you type?" he asked. "I've got a whole wad of manuscript."

I scented a Somerset Maugham or James Laver story.

Unluckily a young Adonis entered the room.

"I've missed my train," she said.

I was quite staggered by his comment.

"When's the next?"

That is not what I was aching to say.

"Eight o'clock," said the enchantress.

"I'll see you off."

"Come again," said the elder. "You liven the old people up."

At that moment the gong rang and I was rejoined by my family.

I ate an enormous helping of chicken and a still more enormous helping of pineapple cream ice.

There was a film that I wanted to see, *Les Enfants du Paradis*. I had booked seats at 1 fr. 80 c. for the 8.30 performance for Jill and myself. Children, as I have said, were not admitted.

Lalage announced that she was going for a walk by herself in the dark. I conjured up visions of abductions and murder. I explained heavily that the Continent, even Switzerland, was not England, and that young girls do not walk alone in the dark.

I left her in a state of sullen sulkiness and found the streets full of young girls walking alone.

The cinema was hot. I watched pictures of starving French refugee children. The audience expressed shock and pity.

Les Enfants started. It seemed a muddled story. The photography was magnificent but I couldn't follow the plot without English captions. I nodded. I fell asleep. I saw the word

ENTR'ACTE. The whole audience rose and went out into the street for air.

Jill saw a man selling chocolates.

"We haven't any sweet coupons," I said.

"Wake up," she said. "You're not in England."

"I'm in dreamland," I said as I munched one bar of chocolate that was mainly honey and another that was all wet.

We returned to our seats. For five minutes I stayed awake. I am told that it was a good film.

As I entered the hotel at midnight I saw one of the white-haired British women carefully roll her newspaper round a stick before going up to bed. I thought of the girl who had missed her train. I echoed the sentiments of the man who had asked her to come again.

I too went up to bed and the next four hours passed in a flash.

Monday, 14th April, 1947

THE birds started to sing even earlier today—at 4.45. As I always wake and work early myself I was glad about that because I like their companionship. They help me to write.

I lay for a little in the darkness, thinking of this and that, but lying awake in the small hours is apt to make them appear very big hours. Time almost stands still, so my method nowadays is to wrap up warmly, sit up in bed, smoke a Havana cigar (two francs) and snuff and write.

I remembered an idea that had struck me last night at dinner, to try each day a new Swiss wine, and give you the benefit of my findings. I began last night with the nearest, but not dearest —it was the cheapest—the white wine known as Vataux-Chillon, a litre of which cost me 3 frs. 80 c. It had a very delicate aroma and certainly was not heady. Imogen who is my wine-taster said that it reminded her of Evian.

"Well, that's what you'd expect," I said heavily. "Evian's just the other side of the water."

The white-haired old lady who kept wrapping her newspaper round a stick looked with disfavour on my winebibber, but I believe it to be good to acquire a sense of taste in the good things of life as early as possible and if wine is not one of the good things of life I should like to know what is.

I wrote till 6.45, got up, shaved and became very impatient because my early morning cup of tea failed to materialise on the stroke of seven. When I am at home I make my own tea, a large pot at four o'clock and drink almost continuously for four hours. At 7.10 it arrived. At 7.20 I had breakfast, not entirely alone. At 7.50 I was waiting for a tram to take me into Montreux. The ticket-collector surveyed my *abonnement* with disapproval and talked volubly. The only way to stop voluble people talking is to offer them an open palm full of money. They immediately smile, pick out this and that coin and perform the service you need.

These *abonnements* (two francs) run out once a day with me and we certainly don't use the tram more than twice, from which you may deduce that tram travel is, like train travel, expensive.

Fumeurs stand awkwardly and bundled very close together at the end of the car with the conductors. Smoking in Switzerland is, I think, frowned on. It is not permitted in cinemas, and it is made uncomfortable for men to smoke in trains. I have never seen a Swiss woman smoking in the streets or on a tram. The men mainly smoke cigars.

I arrived in the chief shopping centre of Montreux just before eight o'clock. Every shop was open. I thought of England and the sweeping outside shops that goes on at nine and thereafter.

My first visit was to Kodak. I was dissatisfied with the way my Leica was working and I wanted a roll taken out, developed and printed and another roll inserted. The girl behind the counter smiled, took away my camera to her father and returned to tell me that my film would be ready for me within twenty-four hours. I found it difficult to believe that after being accustomed to wait over a month in England. I wanted a fresh roll and fell for a new gadget, a box of ten rolls at 27 frs. all done up together with a tongue sticking out.

Father and daughter were both lengthily rhapsodical. The Swiss are perfect salesmen because they all obviously love the goods they sell.

I went off to the Libraire Payot to buy yet another map and secured an excellent road map of the whole country for 3 frs. 75 c. I then tried out a number of fountain-pens, but as I am only completely at home with a Schaeffer I resisted the new stream-lined Parkers and Eversharps and went over to look at the books. I was delighted to find paper editions of R. C. Hutchinson. I

regard him as one of the outstanding novelists of our time. My
eyes then fell on a limp leather-bound diary, with extremely
smooth thin pages which had been reduced because the year was
so far advanced. Realising suddenly that my wife was taking no
notes I bought it for her at 7 frs. 50 c. I then bought some
brillantine at 3 frs. 50 c. and went in search of the tobacconist
who had sold me Havana cigars enclosed in silver and gold tubes,
over the possession of which Lalage and Imogen had both
fought, at 1 fr. 75 c. and 2 frs. each. I mistook his shop and was
led into buying a much smaller cigar in another shop at 2 frs.
I then found a chocolate shop, the Villars, where I bought 500
grams of the best assorted chocolates that I have ever eaten for
5 frs. 65 c. There was a generous proportion of liqueur-filled
chocolates in the bag which I knew would appeal to Imogen.
Even in Switzerland shopping takes time and I was still at it
when the clock struck nine. We had been told to be ready for our
Gruyère excursion by 9.15 and as luck would have it there was
a much longer interval than usual between trams. In point of fact
I regained the Bonivard at 9.14 to find my family sitting in the
sun on the terrace and to my surprise almost ready. I displayed
my purchases and as usual incurred the wrath of Lalage who
saw nothing but wild extravagance in the diary but was mollified
by the sight of the chocolates. Imogen produced my letters, each
of which bore a surcharge stamp of five cents. As there were a
number of bills among them I began to doubt whether I had
been wise in having them forwarded.

As the sun promised to be glaring I went upstairs in search of
my skiing cap to protect my eyes. I disapprove of sun-glasses
because I like to see the natural colours with the naked eye, however fierce the light. Sun-glasses always give me the impression
of approaching thunder. I dislike them on women, but I
imagine them to be a great promoter of virtue, for no woman in
glasses has ever aroused in me the sort of appeal that virtuous
women are supposed to resent, and sun-glasses completely obli-
terate the face.

At 9.40 a swarthy motor-coach driver ran up the drive to
announce that the coach to Gruyère awaited us below.

I swaggered down, feeling immensely proud of myself in my
skiing cap which bears the badge of the Oxford University Ski
Club which is obtainable at the cost of a shilling for anyone who

cares to buy one. I had not encountered any other Englishman in a ski cap and as I always like to be different I was glad about that.

In spite of the fact that there was every evidence of the temperature becoming torrid I was wearing a thick woollen vest, red woollen shirt and winter suit, a red woollen waistcoat, an ordinary waistcoat, a sheepskin waistcoat, a heavy R.A.F. overcoat and a woollen scarf.

My appearance must have excited the thirty or so waiting occupants of the motor-coach. But with the hood off at five thousand feet . . . well, you never know. I had been bitterly cold in spite of these wrappings in Devon last August. I prefer being baked to being frozen.

I was extremely glad that I had had the foresight to pay an extra franc apiece for the four of us to occupy the front row of seats. By so doing I not only ensured the perfect view but also ensured against draughts which invariably give me a cold. I didn't look at my fellow passengers but I soon heard enough to know that Lancashire and Yorkshire were as usual in the lead. I also gathered that mine were not the only children.

We set off past the Castle of Chillon towards the Rhône valley, the driver talking as fast as he drove in French to Lunn's guide who was sitting by his side. He rose at intervals to point out this and that, but as he didn't spell the names of the places I was more often than not none the wiser.

The first thing I noticed about the Rhône valley was its width and fertility. It is of course flat and the alluvial is rich. The feathery trees soon gave place to trim orchards, and at Yvorne I saw a white castellated château on the hillside and many more steeply set vineyards on the hillside, each occupying about half an acre and bounded by a limestone wall.

Lunn's man rose to tell us that Yvorne produced the best wine in the canton. I made a mental note of that. Yvorne for me that night if I could remember.

The valley closed in and we came to the medieval castle of Aigle, converted, we were told, into a prison. The Swiss flag hung limply from the tall tower. Lunn's man commended the Aigle wine and announced the fact that this was the site of the Montreux golf club. There seemed to me to be no spare room for a golf-course except on the precipitous sides of the Alpine crags.

The Swiss, I felt, are not at all the sort of people to devote to a mere game land that could be profitably developed for pasture or vineyard.

We passed a large number of carts. I saw no idlers. Everyone was at work in the fields or on the road.

We turned aside from the Rhône past the tall spire of Aigle church to begin our long and winding climb of the mountains.

We were shown the place where the famous Hôtel des Bagnes had stood before troops had been billeted in it and I began to look over the edge of extremely low stone walls into precipitous ravines. The driver took his corners fast, once a little too fast for a descending car which was being driven with equal speed. There was some backing and an exciting exchange of wordy but not vituperative French. We looked across the narrow gorge at a viaduct which we were told had a span of two hundred and forty feet.

We came to Visarguy and saw pillboxes above the road which inspired our guide to tell us that the whole of the road had been mined and the neighbouring hills tunnelled during the war.

"How," asked Imogen, "did the people in the chalets get down for food if the roads were mined?"

"They're self-supporting," I answered. "They could last out a year."

"The war lasted for six years," she reminded me sternly.

"They must have gone over the top or round," I said.

I looked down on an attractive power-house at the foot of the ravine and immense pipes climbing the opposite hillside.

"Electric-power schemes," I said, "don't always disfigure the landscape."

"It depends on the size of the landscape," said Lalage.

Lunn's man pointed ahead to the mountains of Chaussi.

"They cut out tunnels to make room for fifteen thousand men there," he said.

"Against the atom bomb?" I asked innocently.

We kept on getting glimpses of the railway-line that runs between Aigle and Diablerets. Then we came to a lovely village clinging to the steep upper slopes of the hill. This was Le Sépey, and far above it I saw the famous sanatorium for the tuberculous at Leysin. Le Sépey has a long narrow street with many attractive hotels overlooking the Dent du Midi. We passed a couple of cyclists pushing their machines up the precipitous road. I realised suddenly why all Swiss bicycles are made of aluminium. One must have featherweights for such steepness. We passed a single bullock being led past a wood-stack. He shied as a horse shies. The chalets on these tops were all curiously carved, with richly coloured shutters and exterior staircases.

Up and up and up we wound our way, the air becoming ever sweeter, and the hairpin bends gave us a grand chance of continually changing our viewpoint.

The towers of Ai rose like mesas above the painted desert and we looked down miles below to the road winding towards Diablerets and Les Pillons, the way to Gstaad.

Tall poles painted red and white lined the road at ten-yard intervals, guide-posts when the snow obliterated the course of the road.

So we came to La Comballaz and the snowfields of the Col des Mosses, the highest point of our journey, five thousand five hundred feet above sea level.

There is a restaurant at the summit, and as the coach drew up I heard the raucous sound from within of Englishmen on holiday.

Believe it or not, but on this perfect sunny day surrounded by Alpine peaks and snowfields on which the hot sun beat fiercely my fellow countrymen were playing bar-billiards.

I discarded two-thirds of my clothes on a table outside the restaurant, ordered a Campari, and began to survey the surrounding hills through my glasses. It always takes me a long time to take in stupendous views.

I first noticed the twin peaks of Tornettaz and the Arnenhorn to the south-west, miniature Matterhorns with tapering spires. Trees clustered to their sides most of the way up the slopes.

"I had no idea that trees grew so high," said my wife. I was watching two birds chasing each other skittishly over the snow.

"I had no idea that magpies lived at five thousand feet," I said.

"Listen," said Imogen.

I listened.

There were larks trilling far up in the sky.

We moved further away from the merrymakers at the billiard-table. A lonely skier shuffled his way slowly over the flat surface of the snow towards the slopes. A man in the distance plodded his weary way over the snow dragging a sledge full of provisions towards an upland chalet. The hillside was dotted with chalets.

The occupants of three motor-coaches sauntered up and down the road while their children chased each other over the snow with snowballs.

I paced up and down in my shirt-sleeves, trying to take the scene in. A very English butterfly fluttered past. More and more larks joined in the heavenly chorus. The mountains to the north betrayed curious parallel perpendicular lines of snow and bare rocklike strips of land that reminded me of Laxton and the Saxon system of tilling.

Long before I was ready we received our orders to repack ourselves into the coach and set off down the hill past great stacks of timber logs. Two walkers sweating in the sun struggled up the hill.

We came to the valley of L'Hongrin where, Lunn's man told us, the Swiss Army would have taken up its stand had it been attacked by Germany. There were pillboxes everywhere and we could see minute entrances to the hill fortifications.

So we came down to the steep gully at L'Etivaz and turned left-handed alongside the river Torneresse.

Quite suddenly we found ourselves looking up the wide green valley of the Tine to the enchanting village of Château d'Oex which looked much larger than it had looked from the train two days before. The valley was completely green.

Lunn's man showed us the ski-hoist (I think he meant ski-lift) and told us that it was the longest in Switzerland, over two miles. I was surprised by the solidity of the houses and the variety of shops in the main street of Château d'Oex.

The girl behind me volunteered the information that there was an open-air swimming-bath. Luckily Imogen failed to hear or we should have had no luncheon.

The coach pulled up outside the door the Hôtel Beau Séjour. The time was 12.15.

"We leave here," said Lunn's man, "at 1.45. Those who have brought packed sandwiches may eat them in the hotel. But the hotel luncheon is excellent."

It was indeed excellent. The proprietor and his wife met us with smiles and appeared to be delighted by my approval of their goulash and recommended me to drink Aigle '45 in preference to Yvorne '44 at six francs a bottle.

There were pink carnations on the table whose aroma was as delicate as that of the wine. I approved of Aigle.

French mustard was produced in a quaint toothpaste tube.

Three sorts of cheese followed—Ton, the local goats' milk cream cheese, Tilsit and Gruyère. We finished the lot and then went to the salon to have coffee under the gaze of a stuffed buzzard. The children went off to play ping-pong while I looked at the mountains.

We left very little time for shopping, but I discovered and bought four exquisitely illustrated books on Alpine birds, Alpine flowers, Alpine animals and Alpine rocks.

We climbed once more into the coach and turning our backs on Gstaad made our way down the cobbled street towards the five-storeyed chalet at Rossinière where Victor Hugo retired to write his memoirs in 1864.

We passed more caves and military hide-outs in the rocks as we drove along the vallley of the Tine. At one place we looked down to a tiny bridge that spanned a ravine and led to a hole in the rock where, according to our guide, a whole hospital and stores had been hollowed out for the Army.

"What will they do with them now?" asked Imogen. "Keep them till the next war, which I hope will never come?"

We passed a second vast and very neat electric-power station, and then ran out of the Canton of Vaud into the Canton of Fribourg.

At Montbovon we watched the railway-line that we had followed two days before. Our way now lay straight ahead into a new country of quite different appearance. The hills fell back to reveal a slice of Normandy, a broad very green plateau of red-roofed clustering villages and prosperous-looking farms.

High on a knoll commanding a view of the whole plateau rose the towers of the Castle of Gruyère, towards which we wound our way, passing an ancient man with an extremely long white beard sitting on the back of a muck-cart. The dusty road wound round and round up the hill towards the castle and suddenly we found ourselves facing one of the most enchanting village streets that I have ever seen.

The street is cobbled and climbs steeply to the castle. It is lined on either side by an unbroken row of joined-up houses with wooden window-frames and balconies carved and painted with dates and coats of arms. Chief among them is the Hôtel de Ville which sports a vast iron sign in gilt and black, bearing the device of a great heron which was the crest of the Lords of Gruyère.

A vast crucifix stood at the top of the street, by the side of which the village women were washing their linen in a stone trough. It was an enchanting, enchanted spot, and I was glad to think we were being given two hours to explore it.

Our guide led us first to see the castle and interpreted in some detail to us all that the French guide so volubly explained to him.

Old men in strange little coloured skull-caps sat on green benches outside the house doors and watched us as we sauntered up the almost tropically hot street.

The Counts of Gruyère, we were told, were at war with the Dukes of Burgundy, and Charles the Téméraire fought with Louis XI. I got more and more excited. I was about to see Froissart come to life.

I saw some chamois heads jutting out from a wall and medieval grotesque gargoyle guttering.

A chestnut avenue led up to the castle gateway.

The guide rang a bell. We entered a courtyard where I read a notice ATTENTION AU CHIEN. There was no dog to beware of, but there was more washing lying in a stone trough. The courtyard was surrounded by carved galleries and had been used in medieval times for plays. On the walls was a coloured mural showing the famous Count Michael, who was a saint, in pursuit of the chamois and finding instead the fair Luce hiding behind a rock. She then became his mistress.

What a superb setting for a historical romance. Ford Madox Ford would have made a memorable story out of this material.

Indeed as I passed from room to room I was living the romance myself.

First there was the cool Gerard Room, with its walls twelve feet thick, huge stone fireplace and granite water-troughs, and beyond it the Hall of Burgundy with pikes and armour and priests' richly embroidered copes and gay silk banners, all relics of the battle in 1470 when the Burgundians were routed and sent home. The transition to the adjoining reception-room was abrupt.

This was a Victorian drawing-room decorated with panels by Corot, a rich medley of flowers and conventionalised figures of maidens painted by him while he was staying here in 1851. These panels are now valued at thirty thousand francs each.

I passed into the Knights' Hall and stood for a long time looking with great pleasure at a number of lively modern murals. The first depicts the arrival of the first Count with his heron, the emblem of the family. It owes its origin to the fact that a heron was the first living creature encountered by the invading host. The second mural depicts the army crossing the Tine, and the third the foundation by the monks of the first Benedictine monastery. The fourth shows the Count setting out for the Crusades, the fifth—the most lurid—shows the helmeted warriors charging with a herd of goats each bearing a lighted torch in his horns to set to flight the Bernese enemy.

Another shows the battle on and for a narrow arrowhead bridge, the next the laying of the foundation-stone, and the last, a vigorous picture of scaling the walls with banners and vast multi-coloured shields, a truly Froissartian picture.

I went into Count Michael's bedroom, hung with vividly coloured Gobelin tapestry which hasn't been cleaned since the sixteenth century.

Our guide told me that two square metres of this tapestry took a year to complete, working ten hours a day.

Leading off it is the smaller bedroom of Michael's fair mistress Luce, who made up in her view of the mountains her lack of tapestry. Her walls are covered with an appropriately feminine quiet linen tapestry which dates back to the fifteenth century.

Enormous cow-bells, hung in the courtyard gallery, aroused the curiosity of a small boy who had failed to show any interest up to that point. We passed a small circular hole in the wall which provided all the light and air that the prisoners were permitted and then descended into the village street once more.

As we passed *l'école primaire* we heard the children chanting in unison, "u-pi-day, u-pi dah." I should have preferred to listen to the bearded Armailli rallying his cattle to the tune of the famous *ranz des vaches*, "Liauba, Liauba, poraria . . ." but that was not to be. On the other hand I got some compensation watching tall, robust bridesmaids in pink organdi, blue satin and yellow marocain emerge from the Hôtel de la Fleur de Lys, followed by the bride in white and the Spanish-looking bridegroom in black.

The old bearded man whom I had seen on the muck-cart limped slowly up to the wedding group, and an obvious spy in white homburg, white mackintosh and sun-glasses, stepped out of an enormous shining Buick.

I went back to the Hôtel de Ville to sit in the shade. The meringues promised by the guide failed to materialise. Instead we had greengages in whipped cream and tea for which we were charged two francs each.

We then set out on a tour of the antique shops and gazed longingly at decorative thick teacups and saucers priced at 8 frs. 75 c. each, at musical boxes, lace doyleys, printed scarves, little skull-caps, embroidered belts and walking-sticks with metal medallions. I was reminded of Zakopane in the Carpathians.

We left Gruyère at 4.45, Imogen nearly missing the bus by going off to gather for us nosegays of anemones and cowslips. All she got for her unselfish act was palpitation and a grazed knee through falling on the cobbles.

We drove through a green land of obvious prosperity. All the boys wore blue smocks. Most of the men were working in timber-yards.

And so we came to Bulle with its wide market-place, medieval castle and ultra-modern skyscraping flats with open balconies. I saw an old lady in a dog-drawn carriage and then we passed the largest timber-yard I have ever seen. The smell of freshly sawn wood followed us for several miles.

At Châtel-St. Denis we halted to inspect a modern cheese factory and exchanged the wood scent for that of cheese in the making. We saw vast copper urns, in which the milk was churned and the hardening rennet added. We saw the presses which squeezed it into discs of three feet diameter and depth of five inches.

We went to the cellars where we watched thousands of cheeses maturing on shelves above an earthen floor, a process that takes about four months. To maintain its crust it is then salted down. We were, to my surprise, presented with no finished sample. That struck me as out of keeping with the Swiss character. Perhaps it was because cheese is rationed.

We set out on the last stage of our journey, and passed out of the Canton of Fribourg into the Canton of Vaud over a bridge.

The country instantly changed.

We exchanged the high flat green rich plateau for a hilly land of high rocks and thick pine-woods.

Soon we were looking down on Lac Léman over miles of vineyards and rich villas. We passed the medieval castle of Bolnay, and drove through the narrow streets of Bolnay village, the houses of which were relatively poor. We came to a bridge that was being repaired and our driver after the usual voluble altercation backed up the hill round several hairpin bends with amazing skill.

And so once more to Montreux after a trip that was well worth the eighteen francs charged for it. I gave the driver two francs tip for the four of us.

I then proceeded to buy fifteen cigars for 27 frs. and 500 grams of mixed chocolates at Villars for 5 frs. 65 c.

At dinner we drank Yvorne at 5 frs. 50 c. a litre and found the bouquet as delicate as but not much better than that of the Aigle of the previous night.

We then set out for the Scala cinema. Above the paybox was a notice forbidding the entrance of any children under sixteen. I presented Imogen (ten) and the ticket-seller grinned and said, "How many?"

"Four at 2 frs. 40 c." I said and we passed in to cushioned seats to see a very large screen and some very dull news which included a bullfight and the Grand National.

Tangier was a spy story told in English with French captions. I made no attempt to follow the very complicated plot but watched the French captions till I fell asleep.

During the *entr'acte* I crossed the road to the Casino and saw a melancholy croupier sitting alone at the gaming tables. I was about to enter the dance hall when the attendant demanded my coat. I let him have it, and was slightly worried by my suit, which was light. The guide had told me that evening dress was not essential but dark clothes advisable.

If I had gone in naked nobody would have noticed for there

was nobody to notice except three sad-looking boys and two women who ought to have been and probably were teachers in an English suburban high school.

There was a dance floor but nobody was dancing. I passed on to the bar. It too was deserted except for three very attractive-looking young women who cheered up immensely at the sight of a rich Englishman. I ordered for myself a Campari and drank it neat. It cost 2 frs. 50 c. I swallowed it quickly, but not before each of the three sirens had sought to gain my favour. I ought to have stayed to talk but my family were waiting in the lobby. I returned to their arms.

" It's a wash-out," I said.

We returned to the cinema and I went on trying to follow the French captions with the aid of the American actors till I fell asleep.

I had enjoyed once more a completely perfect day.

Tuesday, 15th April, 1947

THE birds began their dawn chorus even earlier and there was every indication that it was going to be a hotter day than ever. In spite of it I not only wore my three waistcoats but I took my heavy R.A.F. overcoat and thick woollen scarf on the day's expedition, which was to Geneva.

We were told to be ready by 8.50. When I got down to break-fast at seven I found a lonely schoolgirl. I invited her to share my table. I learnt that it was her last day out of six. She still had three to go in Paris but she was full of regrets. It had apparently grieved her very much to see such lovely alluring things in the shops and not be able to buy them. Otherwise her holiday had been perfect. She was one of a large group brought over by her form-mistress, who apparently made a general prac-tice and presumably a profit out of it.

The coach arrived on time. We were the first to be picked up.

At the Beau Rivage we were joined by our guide who announced that owing to a mistake in the bookings there would be no room for him and we should have to get on as well as we could with the Swiss driver who hadn't a word of English. We went round the town picking up more and more passengers. That took just an hour. Two badly printed broadsheets containing a brief description of the itinerary were handed round. According to the itinerary we were to encircle the lake.

"Goody, goody," said Imogen.

According to the itinerary we were to encircle the lake in a left-handed circle.

"Bad luck," said Lalage who was sitting with Jill on the left-hand side.

We passed a sweep on a bicycle wearing a top-hat.

"Good omen," said Jill.

The coach made a right-hand turn and we set off along the shores towards Lausanne.

"For us," I said.

"We'll be coming back the other way," said Jill hopefully.

"Not if it says so in the itinerary," I said.

I was right.

The road was wide, the surface perfect. The day was cloudless. We had the front seats. I loosened my waistcoat buttons. The passengers in the rear felt a draught. The roof was drawn two-thirds along. I was still in the sun and liking it.

"My coffee," said the passenger behind me, "was thick for the first time today."

"What time do we start back?" asked her companion.

I wondered why the English ever come to Switzerland. I looked out on the lake. I saw a white house in a tiny island a hundred yards off the shore with a small yacht lying at anchor in between.

"That's not a desert island, is it, Daddy?" asked Imogen.

"About as deserted as Park Lane," I replied.

All the houses that lined the lake were substantial and very rich-looking. All had gardens stretching down to the beach.

We drove along the *quai* at Vevey where we watched the Swiss women with huge baskets buying vegetables and flowers in the open-air market, the booths of which were covered with gaily coloured huge umbrellas. I saw a medieval castle on the lakeside but there was no guide to tell us anything about it.

The hillside above us was entirely filled with walled-in strips of vineyards in most of which men were working.

The tall protecting wall between the road and the lowest vineyard was a blaze of yellow and purple saxifrage. Passers-by were warned not to pick the flowers. We came to a triangular notice

bearing simply an exclamation mark. It struck me as neater and
more explicit than our parallel notices about DANGER—ROAD UP.
That was the only obstruction we encountered in a hundred and
twenty miles and the surface of the road was everywhere perfect.
How is that achieved?

Occasionally among the vineyards I saw a château or a farm.
I felt a strong desire to visit one of these and see how wine was
made. Imogen must have guessed my thoughts.

"How is wine made, Daddy?" she asked.

"You see those millions of short sticks?" I asked.

"I can't see anything else," she said. "Why do they have to
have so many new ones?"

"Probably the Swiss love of cleanliness," I said.

"What do they do with the old ones?" she asked, pointing
to neat stacks of old ones (is "boles" the word?) lying by the side
of the walls.

"Firewood or museums, I suppose."

"Does the vine grow up the pole?"

"That is the idea."

"How long?"

"In time or length?"

"Both."

"Well, it's now April and all the poles are bare, so presumably
the vine is now a seed in the earth. I don't know. Most of the
vines at home are in greenhouses and are quite old trees which
bear fruit year after year."

I was getting muddled.

"Anyway," I went on hurriedly, "when the grapes come."

"At what time of year?"

"I don't know."

"You don't know much."

"I know that I like their taste when they are pressed into
wine."

"Why do the grapes of different vineyards taste different?"

"The skill of the grower, the type of plant, the type of soil,
the strength of the sun, the date of picking, the process of pressing. All those things . . ."

"Aren't you clever."

"Writers have to be clever. They have to keep on inventing."

"Are you inventing?"

"I certainly am."

"May I have a chocolate?"

"Take two."

"Thanks piles."

We saw a field of tulips in full flower and came to Lutry. I gazed at a round fat Norman tower among the vineyards, zig-zag green-and-white painted shutters on a chalet and a castle with strong prison bars across its windows.

There were tulip trees and American-currant bushes in full flower.

Bedding hung out of all the chalet windows. We came to Lausanne shining in the sun. There were a park and gardens with smooth lawns with masses of daffodils in flower leading down to the lake on which I saw half a dozen steamers at their moorings and many little boats. The hotels that faced the lake were palatial. I was reminded of Los Angeles. We passed sky-scraping ultra-modern flats each with its own balcony on which people were working, eating and playing.

We passed a very old tiny church and a cemetery arranged in symmetrical rectangular blocks the graves of which were a blaze of multi-coloured spring flowers. It looked very gay.

In a few minutes we were in open country with very green smooth fields on either side and many cherry orchards. The whole countryside sparkled in the sun. We passed a dogs' home which seemed an anomaly, for I didn't pass six dogs in the whole of those hundred and twenty miles.

We passed another huge castle on the lakeside and came to Morges which has a large factory outside which were stacks of barrels. Even the barrels were painted in all the colours of the rainbow. There was also a large timber-yard.

The main street was colourful owing to the display of bright yellow sun-blinds which had been drawn over most of the shops. Morges too has a green, and this green was covered with washing hanging out to dry. Then followed some woods and so we came to St. Prex with its thin-spired church and more vineyards. There was a cyclists' track on both sides of the road, which was perhaps as well, for our driver who drove very fast and with great skill disregarded cyclists of whom there were quite a number.

Of cars there were remarkably few. We came to Rolle with

a medieval castle on the shore and then to my surprise the driver drew up at the entrance to a pleasant square white house with bright green shutters protected on the east and west by trees on the lakeside.

The passengers woke up.

"Shushill," said the driver.

I had been prepared to be shown the home of Madame de Staël, Voltaire, Gibbon and even Calvin, but not "Shushill." I felt very ignorant of Swiss history.

It was not till I heard someone at the back say, "Winston certainly knows how to pick 'em," that I realised that I had been looking at Churchill's Swiss country home. He certainly knows how to pick them.

There was a paddock with a horse in it, a poultry-run with turkeys (the only turkeys I saw in all Switzerland), men muck-spreading in the grass, and other men stripped to the waist ploughing.

We passed a number of very handsome' country houses, a hospital, a radio station, and several castles, the most imposing being that at Nyon, above the turrets of which floated a banner of green and white.

Nyon also boasts a *plage,* prosperous farms, a few vineyards, and a large square house on a hill.

We had stopped at Rolle to admire Winston Churchill's house. Nobody asked the driver to stop at Coppet to visit the home of Madame de Staël. We are an insular race.

At Versoix there were several houses to let or sell. I was surprised because we were within sight of Geneva where I had been told there was no vacant room to be had in any hotel till October.

We were taken a little way from the main track to halt outside the glittering white buildings of the League of Nations. Enthusiasts dismounted to take photographs of it.

We drove on to a high bridge, the Pont Butin, and looked down on the Rhône. There were council houses near by with all their bedding hanging out of the wide open windows.

We saw the spire and two towers of the Cathedral of St. Pierre rising high above the city and drove on down past a farm which was practically in the town and many spacious villas to cross the Rhône again at a lower level, and then dismounted to

look at the Reformation memorials put up in 1936 to commemo-
rate the quatercentenary of Calvin. I took a photograph of the
group of reformers, Calvin, Farel, Beza and Knox. There were
smaller effigies of Cromwell and Roger Williams, and the Lord's
Prayer was engraved on the stone in many languages. This monument is in a large park. The driver had conveyed to us the idea
that he would meet us at the further end. Only a handful of us had
been sufficiently interested in Calvin to make the excursion. We
were ill rewarded, for after waiting in vain under a torrid sky at
the appointed rendezvous one of our party went off in search of
the coach and found it hidden in a by-street.

I was content watching the English girls employed by the
League of Nations or UNO going off to lunch. I was struck by
the extreme smartness and elegance of the women who were not
English and I suddenly remembered roads bearing the notice
TO PARIS and the fact that we were on the French border.

Geneva isn't Swiss at all. It looks like Paris, smells like Paris,
and dresses and behaves like Paris. I had left the land of
geniality and courtesy. I was back among the French.

We drove on through handsome streets of amazingly fine shops
to the Quai Qaciz, and looked out over the enormous harbour. In
the far distance rose the white peak of Mont Blanc.

There was an open-air café just by the car park. The driver
conveyed the joyful information that we were free till 4.15 and I
hurried to seize a seat in the café, took off my coat and all my
waistcoats and sat in my shirt-sleeves to unpack my packed
lunch.

It was a revelation. My bag contained two boiled eggs,
varieties of meat in sandwich rolls, a whole box of Berinne
cheese, an orange and an apple. The rather melancholy but business-like garçon appeared. We settled down to a Gargantuan
feast. I drank tomato juice, two Camparis and ended with a
coffee ice.

Lalage and Imogen had two milk-shakes (*frappés*) and drank
them dreamily through a straw. I then sensed something wrong.
Both the children complained of feeling sick. I tried to induce
them to sit in the shade. They lost interest in Geneva. I have
never seen greed so quickly rewarded. I was feeling none too
good myself. I made pious resolutions which I knew I should not
keep.

The native sitters in the sun regarded us with amusement.

The garçon handed me a bill for 13 frs. 50 c. and refused my voucher.

We staggered across the flower-bedecked park (mainly yellow pansies) towards a cigar-shop. I looked enviously at a Rolex watch which didn't need winding up, at another of those watches that tell everything up to the phases of the moon, and then crawled up steep steps to the Cathedral which looks most imposing outside.

Whatever else you do in Geneva don't waste time on the Cathedral.

I ought to have known better. It bore, of course, the stamp of Calvin.

In all this land of prodigal beauty Geneva Cathedral was the only thing of repulsive ugliness that I had seen. Man had built to the greater glory of the God who created the Alps this ignoble mortifying monument. There was nobody in it except a photographer on a high scaffolding taking photographs of the gargoyles. It is the only cathedral in the world that I have ever seen which attracts, and rightly attracts, no visitors. It is the only cathedral that I know of where they charge an entrance fee. I bitterly resented the waste of twenty-five cents and Lalage read me a well-deserved lecture on extravagance.

We passed the Hôtel de Ville, descended the hot street on the shady side to the Musée Reth where we saw a vast crowd ascending the steps to see the exhibition of a hundred and seventy-two pictures by Van Gogh. The entrance fee here was two francs. It could have been two hundred francs and would still have been worth it.

I recovered my equanimity on the instant as I gazed on these exquisite, colourful and most understanding interpretations of life.

What did I like best? What a silly question. Yet I asked it of Imogen and Lalage.

" I liked the pair of old boots and the pair of old shoes," said Imogen. " You could see the people in them."

Lalage thought that Van Gogh had wasted much too much paint.

" He laid it on much too thick. If he was so poor how could he afford it?" she asked.

It seemed a reasonable question.

Imogen was more interested in his ears.

"He keeps on painting himself side-face," she said. "I want to see his poor ear."

I showed her the one with the ear bandaged.

"Poor man," she said, "I do feel sorry for him."

"You needn't," I said. "He knew that he was a great genius."

"Do geniuses always know?" she asked.

I thought of myself and Swift.

"Always," I said.

The exhibition was packed out, but very few of the Van Gogh lovers were British.

It was like looking at the Alps. I couldn't take in a hundred and seventy-two pictures at one go. I walked round and round the galleries, halting in front of the portrait of the old man with his head buried in his hands as he sat forward in the cheap cane chair. That seemed to me to express what the artist was trying to express well nigh perfectly. I paused before his deep blue skies above the golden harvest-fields before a storm, and admired his boldness of colour.

Everything that he touched he adorned and he gave significance to everything. The candle on the yellow chair meant so much more than a candle on a yellow chair. Jill approached me to ask me if he had ever been to China.

Jerked out of my mood I answered angrily.

"Did he? I couldn't care less."

I was looking at a flask of wine and some apples. I turned to a picture of a narrow cobbled street with café tables and lights with the cobalt blue of a starlight night above. Then from a singularly graceful nude I turned to a landscape of vivid green roofs, white crazy broken-down cottages, a young boy cutting corn with a sickle ...

Everywhere there was beauty. The sense of colour was overwhelming.

I went out into the hot afternoon sun, dazzled. I noticed a lot of attractive young girls whose skirts were too short (I didn't mind that) and whose hair was too long (I didn't mind that either). I like to see a lot of leg when it is a shapely leg. I like to see a lot of hair when that hair is glistening in the sun. Many young wives passed, all in silk stockings, all in extremely smart coats and skirts and hats.

They were indeed elegant, but they lacked something that Van Gogh possessed in profusion. Was it vitality or was it vision?

I passed on to the shops, refrained with difficulty from buying a calfskin brief-case for ten pounds and agreed with Jill that we all except myself needed thick white woollen socks and stockings. My need, she told me, was handkerchiefs. I acquired six Pyramid handkerchiefs at two francs each.

I had a glass of tea without milk and refused caviare at eight francs.

I sat on a seat overlooking the harbour and sympathised with Imogen in her desire for a bathe.

At 4.15 we rejoined the motor-coach. Nobody was late.

We set off for home, not round the south side of the lake as the programme foretold, but back by the route along which we had come. Jill was annoyed. I was pleased. I now had the lakeside window and I wanted to ratify, confirm or correct a few first impressions.

We drove along the quai with hundreds of drinkers in the sun on my left and Mont Blanc hazy, mysterious and very white high up on my right and far away.

Lalage settled down after her invariable custom in coach or train to make notes for her diary. She observes very carefully and has a most appreciative eye, but is seldom voluble. She prefers writing her opinions.

We passed the British Consulate and a plaque to Woodrow Wilson, a very flamboyant memorial to somebody and thousands of flowers in their quayside beds.

Imogen saw somebody bathing.

" Can we, when we get home?"

I thought it unlikely that night.

" Tomorrow," I said. " If——"

I watched more men ploughing stripped to the waist and thought how fit a subject they would have made for Van Gogh.

We passed Churchill's house without stopping this time and looked across to Grenoble from Rolle.

We passed restaurants every mile or so and I longed to pull up at each of them. I was getting thirsty. We looked across the bay to Lausanne and turned aside at Morges to see the Arsenal and another angle of Mont Blanc. There was, curiously enough, no sign of anybody bathing.

"Sun-bathing hill is a good phrase," said Imogen who was reading the itinerary guide.

"It is not only good. It's true," I said looking out over the baked vineyards.

Time flew as we drowsily drove in the glare of the sun. I woke up to find myself in the upper part of Lausanne, a place of sky-scrapers and crowded streets.

"There's a Dragon," said Imogen, "on a bike."

The phenomenon was a small boy who was at her preparatory school.

We ran alongside a railway-line but I saw no trains. There were trolley-lines but no trolleys. We passed an extremely hand-some elementary school and admired the red spires of the cathe-dral, the wonderful post-office that seemed to be all glass, and the luxurious Palace Hotel.

Imogen pointed to a sign.

"Old India," she said. "That's a tearoom."

She had been reading her guide-book with profit.

We ran into a narrow bottleneck at Les Torrents. Our driver took it at top speed expecting and luckily meeting with no resis-tance.

We came to more vineyards. The whole steep hillside was covered with rows of short poles and the high sea-wall was covered with rock plants. We were once more at St. Saphorin which I am told retains its old seventeenth-century habits as well as its old-world atmosphere.

As we passed the diving-board at Vevey and saw again the white square house islanded in the lake and the glittering white houses of Montreux set below the high Alps I agreed with Imogen that our end of the lake was far preferable to the Geneva end. We had become violent partisans.

Montreux is much quieter and much more beautiful than Geneva.

We got off the coach at the Hôtel Eden and I went to claim my first lot of films. We shrank almost visibly when we learned that I had unwittingly been using colour films. The whole lot were ruined. I tried to be stoical but I took Jill's blame badly. I recovered a little on acquiring 500 grams of mixed chocolates at Villars where the smiling woman said that the people of Geneva were too French for her liking, too brusque. I couldn't agree more.

I recovered still more as we sat outside the Metropole and drank two Camparis with vermouth.

But my nerves were still sensitive.

When Jill abused me for paying 2 frs. 40 c. for seats at the Apollo Cinema instead of 1 fr. 80 c., I said, "It was you who objected to hard seats."

Lalage volunteered the remark that people were happy when they were first married.

That made me so angry that I refused to sit with the family when we boarded the tram. I stood by myself among the *fumeurs* though I was not myself smoking.

The beauty that surrounded me as dusk fell completely restored my sense of harmony.

Pinpoints of light flickered from white chalets high up on the hills. The snowclad peaks were tinged with rose-pink. The lower slopes were black as Acheron. The lake was a still glossy blue-black mirror.

I drank St. Saphorin at five francs a litre and could hardly restrain my merriment when Lalage spilt the bottle over the table.

It has a delicate aroma but is not quite in the same class as Yvorne, or am I imagining that? I ate voraciously.

We went back to the Apollo Cinema, to the children's delight.

As soon as I heard the voice of Sir Aubrey Smith I went to sleep.

At the *entr'acte* I woke up.

Jill said, "Can you snore less loudly?"

I got up. "I'm going home," I said and walked out into the night.

I walked down to the waterfront. I had it to myself except for one young girl who was leaning over the railings smoking. I resisted a strong desire to talk to her and admired the more satisfying loveliness of the lake.

I sauntered into the Casino, resisted the doorman's attempt to rob me of my coat, found a dozen couples dancing and went on to the bar to order myself an orange squash.

A neighbouring siren smiled her metallic smile. I was not interested.

The cabaret girl, dressed in almost nothing, gave me a gay smile.

"Give her a drink," I said to the barman.

"She likes champagne," he said.

"Don't give her a drink," I said, thinking of Lalage.

I watched her do her act. She was vivacious and kicked high as she ogled the surrounding old men.

I walked out and boarded a tram.

The hotel lights were out.

I went quickly to bed.

Wednesday, 16th April, 1947

I HAVE made a discovery which should prove useful to burglars. People are woken less easily by light than by noise. This book could never be written unless I write it each day, and the only free time I have is between three o'clock and eight o'clock in the morning.

My wife is alas a light sleeper and has a quite understandable objection to being roused as early as three o'clock. If I make the slightest noise she wakes and urges me with some heat to exercise a little consideration for her tired self and lie still in the darkness.

This I find impossible. Ten minutes of lying in the dark in the early hours is to me a lifetime of boredom. On the other hand my brain at this hour is at its most lively and I am quite happy to be working, but to work I must have light. After many experiments I have discovered that if I put out my manuscript-block and notebook, bottle of Evian, cigar and snuffbox the night before, I can turn on the light at three o'clock without causing her to do more than grunt and turn over.

This morning after I had finished my work I got down to breakfast at seven o'clock and found as usual that I was not alone. There was the usual sprinkling of foreign men all with pink packages of packed lunches getting ready to go off into the mountains.

At nine o'clock Lunn's man appeared and I prepared to pay for pleasure past. He began by asking me what was the half of 7 frs. 70 c. which led me to wonder how he did his bookkeeping.

He handed me a slip of paper and I handed him vouchers

for two hundred francs. The Gruyère excursion had cost eighteen francs each for the motor-coach, half-price for Imogen (ten), but full fare for Lalage (fifteen). The lunch at the Beau-Séjour at Château d'Oex had cost six francs each.

The Geneva excursion had also cost eighteen francs each for the motor-coach, and when I told him that I had been informed that a taxi for four would have cost less he told me that the taxi fare for that journey was a hundred and forty francs.

I told him that I intended going by funicular and train to Rochers de Naye in the afternoon and he immediately produced tickets for that, the return fare for which was 7 frs. 70 c., Imogen to be the half of that. We arranged to go to Champéry the next afternoon and by way of the luxurious Red Arrow to the Blue Lake and Interlaken on the Saturday.

At ten o'clock he very kindly accompanied us on a morning's shopping expedition.

As Imogen was determined to bathe, and the day was obviously going to be hot and cloudless, I suborned him to walk behind with her to tell her that the lake was practically bottomless and therefore far colder than the sea in England.

We came first to a shop displaying Brazil nuts.

" What are those queer-looking things ?" asked Imogen.

A sense of the deprivation that children had been called upon to endure during the last six years suddenly overcame me. I bought 500 grams for 2 frs. 50 c. We cracked them on the pavement. She forgot all about the bathing in her excitement.

" Mighty fine," she said. " Mighty fine."

We entered a draper's shop. For the next half-hour we turned over a variety of bathing-costumes utterly different from and aesthetically infinitely more attractive than any that I have ever seen in England. Imogen's final selection was a criss-cross mesh of scarlet and white at eight francs. Lalage and Jill decided on a royal-blue background with a number of white cranes embroidered all over it. These cost twenty-three and twenty-eight francs respectively. It was a great triumph at last to have prevailed upon Lalage to accept anything. She denies herself everything so that the rest of us can indulge in luxuries.

We then had a brief respite from shopping while I sought to make up for the disappointment of the lost film by taking some thirty photographs of the family against a background of lake and town and shop and Alpine heights. They were very patient and hugged their bathing-costumes.

We then entered a chemist's for a purpose that I have forgotten and I emerged the richer by a nylon hairbrush at ten francs and a nailbrush at four francs. I then proceeded to a shop where the family went crazy over musical boxes and I took the opportunity to acquire surreptitiously a pocket-knife at 10 frs. 50 c. that simply bristled with the sorts of gadgets that might come in useful if I ever bought a horse.

I then found it necessary to call on the bank as I had run out of vouchers. To my surprise I found it closed. The hour was 12.15. They close from twelve to two. As I had completed my roll of film I called on Kodak and was asked to return in twenty-four hours for the finished product. I hardly dared hope that I should not again draw blank.

After our labours we sat in the sun outside the Metropole drinking Campari and vermouth and returned to the Bonivard at one o'clock to find that all the other guests had finished. I imagine that a gong is rung at 12.15 or 12.30 and most of the English visitors make a point of being in to lunch and also of being punctual.

At 1.50 we set off on foot for Territet to take the funicular. There are two funicular stations at Territet and we stood for some time expectantly outside the one marked Mont Fleuri. It looked deserted and forbidding. I went in search of the other and found a bright sunlit station made still more bright by a number of very artistic and colourful posters advertising other resorts in Switzerland. There were perhaps a dozen other would-be passengers, among them the two girls from Cambridge who had shared our compartment from Victoria to Folkestone in the far distant dark ages of last week.

They too looked transformed and almost unrecognisable.

After looking up the steep railway-line we all agreed that it was exciting, formidable and at least twice as long as the funicular that links Lynton and Lynmouth.

We entered our carriage and the discussion turned to shopping. I learnt to my surprise that the girls had been warned by Lunn not to exceed an expenditure of five pounds.

That seemed to me very odd, in view of the explicit statement about a limit of seventy-five pounds issued by the Government.

The doors were locked and we glided very slowly upwards. At once we passed into a country of colourful wild flowers which Imogen tried to pick as we climbed. I was pleased to see that she wasn't in the least frightened. Lalage on the other hand was concentrating on the approaching down car.

"We shan't pass it at the junction," she said. "It's much further away."

But her fears were groundless. We did.

Within ten minutes we were at Glion where we changed trains and joined an army of skiers, two of them very small children in scarlet skiing tunics, trousers and caps.

The train from Montreux came in, already overcrowded. We stood among a group of voluble Swiss girl skiers and began a stiff winding, crawling journey, threading our way among chalets perched precariously on the steepest of slopes, among mountain tracks that dived through woods and along the mountainsides.

Intermittently we got magnificent glimpses of the lake far below and of the streets of Montreux. We came to the snow line and passed through a number of tunnels.

High wooden fences lined some parts of the track to keep the snow back.

We looked across a ravine to see the first avalanche of our tour. I could not hear its thunderous roar, but I could see the dirty brown of the earth mixed with the foaming white of the pure snow. Imogen was duly impressed.

"Suppose an avalanche falls on the train," she said.

"It would be just too bad," I said, "but also very unlikely."

"Why?" she asked.

I went into a detailed explanation of northern and southern slopes.

We stopped at Caux where somebody volunteered the information that all the hotels had been bought up by the Oxford Group.

In answer to a question from Imogen I explained that the Oxford Group had nothing to do with Oxford.

"They just took the name in order to impress people like you."

"But I'm not impressed," she said.

"You can't tell how glad I am about that," I said, and fell quite suddenly asleep.

I was told that I had missed a lot of scenery and created quite a diversion by my snoring.

"They thought you were an avalanche," said Imogen when I woke up.

We were by that time entirely surrounded by deep snow and still climbing steeply. We came to a band of skiers and saw far above us a palatial hotel perched just below the summit of a precipitous peak.

"There," I said, "is Rochers de Naye."

I looked out on a world of snowy peaks.

"We're six thousand feet up," I said.

"How do you know?" said Imogen.

"My heart and ears tell me so," I said.

"How?"

"My heart is pumping a thousand to the minute and I can't hear. My ears are full of cotton-wool and buzzing."

I watched a procession of skiers being hauled up a ski-lift.

Very soon we were at the station and joined the procession through a slush of mud and snow.

Most of the passengers made for the hotel. I saw a narrow track of earth along the extreme edge of the precipice leading to the top. That was the way for me.

Saying nothing to the others I started to climb. It was only when I had gone within an ace of slipping over the edge that I regretted that I was wearing thin suède shoes with soles smooth enough for dancing. With thick nailed boots I could have taken the climb in my stride, but the hot sun had made the going impossible. I sat down in the moist earth and nearly cried. I knew that a superb view awaited me just above from the concrete platform that crowned the summit and it had suddenly become inaccessible.

I started to slip down on my bottom, and was surprised to see Lalage, Imogen and Jill just below. As I didn't want them to be disappointed I said as I passed, "It's my heart. I'm going to sit down for a bit. You go on."

They went on.

Suddenly I heard a cry from above. It was Jill.

"I feel sick," she said. "Literally sick."

I looked up to see that she was really sick with fright, but as she wouldn't make her clothes dirty she wouldn't come down on her hands.

The children were completely unperturbed but slipping badly.
I put on the voice that admits of no argument.
" Come down," I said.
They came down.
We all descended to the concrete platform outside the hotel
that overlooked the skiing slopes.
There was plenty of activity.
" It looks simple," said Jill.
" I'm glad you think so," I said.
" I want to put on my bathing-suit," said Imogen.
I helped her to disrobe.
Our fellow travellers looked surprised.
If she couldn't bathe in the bottomless lake Imogen had de-
cided that she could sun-bathe on the giddy heights.
She ran over the snow in her scarlet and white bathing-suit
and forgot the absence of water.
A number of visitors went indoors to have tea. I was looking
for an alternative way up to the top.
" I shan't be long," I said to Jill.
" Don't do anything silly," she said.
" Trust me," I said.
I began travelling along the snow slopes in my thin shoes
towards the ski-lift. I sank in to my knees and wondered whether
I was about to start an avalanche.
I reached the ski-lift and then began to make a zigzag path
towards the grassy patch under the summit. To the great indig-
nation of my heart I did this fast. I was anxious not to start
anything.
The half-dozen people on the summit looked down on me with
disfavour. I knew what they were thinking. They had come up
the long arduous way. I was cheating. I wanted to point out to
them that they were all wearing climbing boots. I was most
inadequately shod for this kind of thing.
I reached the top and found myself looking down a precipice
six thousand feet to the lake.
It was a stupendous view.
A honeymoon couple had left the platform and sat on the
very edge of the precipice, with their arms round each other's
waists. I tried to take in what lay before my eyes. It was quite
impossible.

A girl by my side said,

" It's impossible to photograph this. It gives you no idea."

" It's impossible," I said, " to describe this. Words give you no idea."

" That's quite right," she said. " You can't communicate it."

" I can't even see it," I said. " I'm just bewildered."

I took out my map and compass and tried to get my bearings.

Immediately below me lay Montreux and the lake which was half-hidden in the haze. I couldn't see more than four miles of shore.

Far in the distance over Geneva rose a long horizontal bank of white clouds.

" The weather's going to change," said the girl.

" Rain always comes up from Lausanne, they say," I volunteered.

" I hope not," she said. " Oh! To be out of England now that April's here."

" Your wish has been granted," I said and walked away.

I didn't want to be reminded.

North-east the land was green and undulating. North I looked up upon a mass of different-shaped peaks. On Dartmoor we pride ourselves on knowing every tor by its shape. Do the Swiss know all the Alpine peaks by name? I doubt it.

There were two vast temple pillars of solid rock untouched by snow, too near the sun I thought for snow. There were two wide green valleys which could be none other than the one leading to Gruyère and the one leading to Gstaad. To the east there was a wilderness of peaks, and to the south I saw the Dent du Midi rising over the wide dark green Rhône valley. To the south somewhere in the haze rose Mont Blanc.

Immediately at my feet were ravines, some wooded, some bare, with streams and pine woods and chalets and waterfalls.

It was all quite indescribable. I just stood and looked.

I wanted to stay there for ever.

Then I saw my darling Imogen's tiny scarlet, almost naked, form darting over the snow far below.

" Daddy," she was shouting.

I no longer wanted to be alone.

I wanted to share my ecstasy with my daughter. I left the platform and started running down the slope, with outstretched arms.

"Here I am," I called.

"Isn't it fine?" she yelled.

"Wizard!" I said.

She ran into my arms, I swirled her round, put her down, and we then joined hands, and ploughed our way downward through the snow.

"Mummy wants her tea."

We reached the platform outside the hotel.

"All the outside tables have been bagged," said Jill.

"We'll go inside," said I.

"On a day like this?" said Jill.

"I'm thirsty," I said.

We found an empty table inside the hotel and I then noticed for the first time what an ultra-modern, practical and dignified place it was.

The woodwork was all carved and very thick.

Imogen wanted an orange juice, Lalage just a piece of bread, Jill a glass of coffee and I a cup of tea. It took a long time to convey these wants to the patient waitress. The total cost was 3 frs. 50 c.

Tea over I bought picture postcards at twenty-five cents each.

Time flashed past. It was 4.30 when we regained the open air to find a huge crowd queuing out of the sun and away from the view on the dark platform for the train which was not due to leave till 5.18.

"I'm going for a walk," I said.

"And lose your chance of a seat."

"I'd rather stand," I said, "for the whole of the rest of my life."

I went off with Imogen to a quiet place on the edge of the precipice where we sat in silence and just looked.

"I can't say anything about this in my diary," said Imogen.

"You're quite right," I said. "Don't try."

"But I want to remember it."

"You'll remember it," I said.

I think she will.

At 5.15 we left an alp that was now wholly quiet and serene and boarded the train. We had of course to stand, but that didn't worry me. At 5.35 we glided out after the ticket-collector had taken our tickets.

I listened to four flushed Swiss girls getting very excited about who should sit and who should stand. Imogen decided that it was imperative for her to go to the lavatory.

"As we're locked in you're going to find it difficult."

I sympathised so deeply with her that I noticed little of the scenery on the way down. The train crawled and the descent seemed interminable.

On our arrival at Glion she made a bolt for her sanctuary and we nearly missed the funicular.

Territet on our arrival seemed as busy as Piccadilly Circus. We walked home where I changed my sodden shoes and socks and then sauntered out to the Taverne du Château de Chillon where Jill and I drank Campari and the children had pink milk-shakes (*frappés*), as we watched the golden ball of the sun cast a golden path over the still waters before it disappeared behind the western hills.

Then well content we walked back along the lizard-haunted path to the hotel and drank a bottle of Villeneuve at five francs. It tasted much the same as all the other local vintages.

After dinner we walked down to the promenade and thence by the footpath along the water's edge under an avenue of weeping willows the whole way to Montreux. There were scarcely any other nocturnal perambulators. A few lovers sat on the benches. A group of raucous East End boys passed cat-calling. We could hear but not see rowers on the lake and saw but didn't hear two silent anglers.

The windows in the hotels and the chalets far above were ablaze with lights.

When we got to the main street we looked at the exterior of Le Perroquet night club and decided against it.

We boarded a tram and by 9.30 I was in bed.

Thursday, 17th April, 1947

I GOT up rather earlier today, 2.30, but out of consideration for Jill I tossed and turned about in the dark for almost an hour before turning the light on to work. I need really not have been so considerate of her feelings. She merely gave a snort when I turned the light on and continued sleeping peacefully till seven o'clock.

I wrote till 6.30 and went down to breakfast at seven o'clock. Now that I had the breakfast-room to myself I had time to realise why I liked it so much. I approved of it first because of its lightness, its enormous windows overlooking the lake, and the lightness of its pale panels and the delicate light sky-blue tinting of the high ceiling. I liked it because of its absolute cleanliness and for the space between and at the tables. I liked it because of the friendliness of the waitresses, most of whom are black-haired, and one of whom excites me. She, like the others, is black-headed, her age perhaps seventeen. She has exquisitely slender legs and she adopts the common habit of wearing a black frock which comes only to a little above her very shapely knees. She is as shy as a fawn but the smile with which she greets my morning salutation is worth swimming across the cold lake to receive. She is not the waitress at my table. I wish she was. We have a secret understanding.

After breakfast I went on working until the hotel came to life and the post arrived bringing Imogen's authorisation.

At 8.30 I went upstairs to find Imogen and Lalage still both asleep, both wearing beatific smiles in a foetid room of closed windows and drawn curtains.

I cannot make them appreciate the joy of waking in fresh air to the sound of the lapping of the lake on the beach.

Our first port of call when we set out was the bank where I discovered that I was allowed to draw only 407 francs in vouchers, that is twenty-four pounds less tax of 8 frs. 85 c. at an exchange of 17.34 to the pound.

After tomorrow I could get more francs, but, I gathered, not many.

This struck me as odd because on my arrival I had only drawn £60, 340 francs in vouchers and 680 francs in cash. That meant that in all I had drawn £84 over here, and £40 in francs at home, that is £124 altogether. I had come armed with £134 in travellers' cheques, so it looks as if I am only allowed to spend £134 altogether. My hotel and travelling bill had come to £126, making a grand total of £260. According to my computation I was allowed £75 for each of us which comes to £300. And I did not realise that I had to deduct hotel and fares from that £300.

I am not a very sound mathematician. I must find out more about the actual facts tomorrow.

At this rate I certainly cannot afford to buy that stop-watch which tells the phases of the moon for 391 francs. I must watch my step even about incidental drinks and chocolates. So far I have had excellent value for all the money I have expended, though I would not say that Switzerland is cheaper than England. The goods are generally in better taste, and what is more important, are to be got without coupons. The little extra tax charged to the foreigner is inconsiderable. I have gone into this question of economics in some detail because it is important that you should know how much you can spend and this was to be a spending morning.

I am not a patient shopper and I take no delight, as Jill does, in spending the whole of a sunny morning going from shop to shop trying on frocks and shoes.

We started by trying to fit out Imogen. This took an unexpectedly long time as the first three shops we tried failed to produce a summer frock that would fit her. Eventually we ran to ground an affair of clean blue and white print which I approved of very strongly, as I approved of its price, twenty-three francs.

Later in the morning I urged Lalage in vain to accept a glorious affair of Cambridge blue and Oxford blue with thick arrows across the breast and hips, in spite of the fact that the price was 108 francs. Jill also failed to find a frock to fit her, not because of prohibitive cost, but of prohibitive hips.

The greater part of their morning was spent in shoe-shops. I had the good sense while this operation was in progress to sit in the sun at a café right on the street and drink Campari.

I got into conversation with a handsome well built man from my hotel who always sat alone and gazed into space.

I learnt from him that he had been left with a war legacy of a diseased lung and sent out here for a year, with a six months' extension. As his pay (he was obviously in the Regular Army) was a mere pittance he lived quietly in a chalet at Montana and only came down to the Bonivard for a special treat.

"I like this place," he said, "for sentimental reasons. When I was a small boy I used to come to Caux with my parents and I used to luge down to Montreux for the daily shopping."

You couldn't luge down from Caux now. There are too many chalets in the way. He told me that he was an author, his subject the psychology of education.

"I write better down here," he said. "The hills always make me restless."

I found that he had come down from Cambridge some five years after I came down from Oxford.

Imogen came to claim me to go back to solve the problem of the shoes, but shamelessly stayed to have a milk-shake (*frappé*).

From the shoe-shop we went to my sort of shop, the stationer's, where I bought for twenty francs a book of superb photographs of the Alps called *Haute Route* and I then dallied with a new streamline Parker fountain-pen which bore a remarkable resemblance to the new Southern Railway engines.

I succumbed to the lure of that at sixty-eight francs and was interrupted by a cheerful fat man from Manchester who sang as he entered the shop and asked me how much duty his wife would have to pay on a five-pound handbag.

I answered, without the book, that if he sang the odds were that the Customs wouldn't even notice it.

I then turned over about fifty purses and notecases and virtuously refrained, with Lalage's aid, from buying any.

Jill then saw some pistachio nut, and cherries coated with chocolate. I asked the price and it seemed reasonable. It was only when I found myself paying thirteen francs for a small bag of each and four sticks of nougat that I realised that I had miscalculated the number of pounds in a kilogram.

The rough working measure for weights is that half a kilogram, 500 grams, approximates to $1\frac{1}{4}$lb. Lalage was almost sick with anger at my extravagance, but regained her equanimity over a milk-shake in the sun outside the Metropole.

Imogen by this time was practically in tears because she had been carrying her new bathing-costume round all the morning but had not been given a chance of bathing. She kept on trying to test the temperature of the water with her hand. She was quite unimpressed by our argument that it was colder in Montreux than in Geneva because we were at the receiving end of the Rhône and that the melting snows came into the lake at our end.

"If it's 65° F.," I said rashly, "I'll bathe."

When that night the hotel porter said that it was only 14° C. she was unable to translate that into terms of Fahrenheit.

The plage at Villeneuve where the Montreux people bathe is not opened until the water registers 17° or 18° C.

But, I thought, there was some slight compensation to be derived from the fact that people are already sunbathing on the plage. From the number of diving-boards strewn up and down the beach it appeared to me that we could bathe anywhere, but perhaps fashion decrees that bathing can only be indulged in from the plage.

"Anyway," I said, "there are some clouds coming up. It'll be too cold if the sky becomes overcast."

After lunch I sank on the terrace into a deep sleep to be woken up by the arrival of the motor-coach due to take us to Champéry.

An extremely fat woman wearing a facsimile of "Edna's fruit hat" sat immovable in the front seat that we had reserved for Imogen. Lunn's man talked of the usual misunderstanding between him and the motor-coach firm.

Imogen sat on Lalage's lap next to the driver and Jill and I sat behind.

As we passed through Villeneuve Imogen looked longingly and with drooping eye at the deserted plage.

"I'd far rather bathe than go for a drive," she said.

It was an unpropitious start.

She sat dripping with the heat in great misery, blind to the beauty of the mountains. A bank of white cloud stood threateningly above the Alps on the left, wisps of white cloud obscured the teeth of the Dent du Midi.

Over the lake the sky was blue.

We passed over a shallow fast-flowing river and saw a number of cement works, and as we came to Noville entered a country of cherry trees weighed down with snow-white blossom. We passed a smithy with coloured tickets of prizes nailed to the door, and then crossed the Rhône, turning down the left bank past more cement works into a land of large crucifixes standing by the roadside. We were in Catholic Switzerland.

Looking across the broad flat grassy valley of rich black alluvial we could see the heights of Naye, and at Vionnez, which has a tall church-spire, the village street was occupied by one girl sitting knitting in the sun.

Here were more orchards on either side of the hedgeless road and men working with the plough. The valley here was about five miles across but it rapidly narrowed to a gorge further on.

We passed another crucifix at the end of an avenue of tall poplars and at Collombey saw horses being shod, some sawmills and another cement works.

The blossom on the cherry trees in the hillside orchard above Monthey looked like ostrich feathers.

At Monthey, an industrial town of white houses on the flat, we turned into the hills on the right and started to climb very steeply along a narrow road with about twenty or thirty hairpin bends. Our driver was unskilful with his clutch and the coach was obviously overdue for the scrap-heap. We passed more and more orchards and little vineyards, and the steep grassy banks were festooned with myriads of anemones and cowslips.

Ahead rose the enchanting village of Trois Torrents, well named, because streams came cascading down steep ravines which we crossed by narrow bridges.

Heavy lorries containing sawn planks kept on meeting us and we or they had continually to back to make it possible for the other to pass.

Trois Torrents is perched precariously on a very steep slope, and its chalets are all decorated with carved wooden balconies and a single crucifix in white or blue.

We were now climbing under the very shadow of the imposing Dent du Midi which rose perpendicularly from the other side of a deep gully.

Groups of schoolchildren accompanied by teachers and nuns edged into the side of the road to let us pass and they all (not the nuns) waved genially and cheered us vociferously. Why don't nuns wave or cheer? I should like them more if they did. Are they subhuman?

More and more white wisps of cloud enshrouded the jagged peaks above the Dent du Midi which stood eleven thousand feet above. More and more schoolgirls waved and cheered. We came to the Val d'Illiez with its fine church and stout decorated chalets and then passed a tall crucifix with a shining gilt carved figure of Christ.

And so to the narrow street of Champéry with its glorious church tower and chalet hotels where we sat on the terrace out of the sun and Imogen pined to see and test the widely advertised magnificent open-air baths while I looked down on tourists sitting below under glass out of the wind in the sun drinking tea and seeing nothing.

We looked out over the wire and ropes of the teleferique or cabin ski-hoist to the mountain-top on our side of the valley. Across the valley I saw green slopes covered with chalets below dense pine woods, above which rose the snow slopes below the grey inaccessible rocks of the cloud-capped Dent du Midi. Just below us scattered over the fields were many chalets with poultry-runs.

Tea arrived with cherry jam and we drank out of cups ringed with an exquisite pattern of wild gentian, rhododendron and primula, the most attractive china that I have ever seen. Imogen kept on peering over the balustrade for signs of bathers and bathing-pools and failed to be convinced when the proprietor assured her that it was much too cold to bathe.

" The Rhône," she said, " doesn't flow up here."

" But the ice melts here," I said.

"What's that got to do with it?" she said. "I want to bathe."

After tea she gained some comfort from climbing into the pulpit of the colourful Catholic Church and declaiming passages from the Bible. She then entered the confessional and spent a long time in silent prayer. I wonder what she found to confess. Was it an inordinate passion for bathing?

She then baptised us all with holy water and said, " I'd rather bathe in that than not bathe at all."

We passed on to the village bazaar, a most enchanting shop which ran along the whole length of one side of the street.

In it we found and tried on floppy straw hats, skiing caps, glengarries in scarlet, little skull-caps, thick white woollen sweaters, black sweaters adorned with figures of chamois, and thick woollen colourful skiing gloves. Jill acquired a pair of these and Lalage as usual refused a pair.

I eyed with envy an alpenstock and a pair of skis. There was also china and a French comic that I bought for Imogen.

As we passed on the church clock struck five. I took photographs, bought postcards and was offered a huge gentian by a tanned lady who went into rhapsodies about the wild flowers she had picked.

We climbed into the motor-coach and began our descent of

the hill, passing fields covered with cowslips, and small girls carrying armfuls of wild daffodils.

I noticed more particularly the rich carving of the chalets, the lantern tower of the church at Val d'Illiez, the small quarter-acre strips of plough at Trois Torrents where we passed more nuns in long white robes and more cheering young girls.

We looked below at a medieval narrow packhorse bridge spanning the gully and I noticed ruefully that our driver failed to slacken speed for a sack-saddled horse that shied badly at our approach. We passed an hotel, the Guillaume Tell (did Tell come from Trois Torrents?), and once more wound our way round the score or so of hairpin-bends towards the Rhône valley at Monthey.

Evening clouds silently gathered above the opposite hills and we looked over the feathery cherry trees to the tall black chimneys of Monthey.

Workmen returning to the hills after their day's work chugged past on motor-bicycles and we came to a land of greenhouses and vegetable gardens.

Just beyond Monthey we turned aside to cross the valley, and I saw to my surprise two separate flocks of sheep, black and white, with young lambs grazing under the island rock of St. Tryphon where a fine château stood in proud isolation perched high above the flat fields.

At Ollon we saw the road to Villars which stands just above, and looking across the Rhône saw the Savoy Alps from a new angle with two black rocks standing above the rest, separated by a huge gap like a toothless jaw.

At Aigle we came back to modernity, large schools, ultra-modern flats, solid stone houses, and a row of houses standing above a vineyard.

And so to Yvorne with its white turreted château and vineyards cultivated right up to the rock face, one of them bearing the words CLOS DE ST. GEORGE in huge letters on its walls.

Here the vast boulders which threatened to fall into the road seemed to me to be of pink granite. But most of the rock hereabouts is limestone.

We passed fields filled with cows weighed down by their heavy bells, and other fields in which well groomed horses were grazing. Two men on Arabs cantered proudly by, and so we came back to Villeneuve where the plage was still deserted, and were put down at the Taverne du Château de Chillon and were warmly greeted by our waitress Hilda who opened the conversation by saying,

"*Il va pleuvoir.*"

I looked up at the quiet sky.

"*Après demain,*" she said.

She was wrong.

Jill's eyes fell on the waitress's shoes. They were the neatest I have seen for years.

Hilda had no English at all, but affability in abundance.

We found out that she bought her shoes in Lausanne. I produced my new streamline Parker pen and began to write.

She produced a similar one with a gold top.

"*C'est très bon,*" she said.

I agreed.

She asked us how long we were staying.

"Till Friday," I said.

Her face fell.

"He means Friday week," said Imogen.

Her face lighted up again.

She was a most engaging and friendly girl. She went off to get our Campari and frappés.

"She's sweet," said Imogen.

For once I agreed that the adjective was appropriate.

We went inside to inspect the lovely prints on the walls. One was of Chillon before the chalets came. Two cows and a horseman were the only occupants of the road. The hills were green and looked as soft as the Sussex Downs. The only other building was the Castle of Bloy. We admired a bold modern painting of a bearded man eating bread and talking to a red-faced monk.

We inspected and approved the solid wooden tables and chairs and the stalls at which diners sat to enjoy their blue trout at seven francs for two pieces, their châteaubriand at fifteen francs for two persons, and their poulet. Hors d'œuvre "riches" cost six francs. I am pretty sure that "riches" was deserved.

The window-boxes were gay with yellow pansies and the terrace filled with couples talking in low whispers as they looked over the romantic castle and still lake.

The radio downstairs was playing dance music. The sky looked serene, and the mountain-tops were silently sinking into their thick bright shrouds.

We walked home along the lizard path to entertain Herr Jenny, the director of publicity of the railways, to dinner. He chose our wine; "A *fendant* for a change," he suggested, and we drank Clos de Montreux and liked it.

He told us that the people of Montreux always called the lake Lac Léman and never the Lake of Geneva "for obvious reasons," but he couldn't tell us the derivation of the word Léman.

He suggested that we should try fondue, a method of eating hot cheese out of a bowl placed in the middle of the table. He advised us to go for nearby walks rather than waste time in his trains going far and tiringly afield.

"Go to Les Avants by train," he said. "See the school of Châtelard and walk down through the woods to Glion to tea and afterwards home."

He explained to the yawning Imogen why she couldn't bathe in the waters of the lake until the temperature rose to 17° or 18° Centigrade.

I took Imogen to bed and quite suddenly realised that we were in for a fierce thunderstorm. Imogen shares my views about lightning and thunder. I shut the windows tight, pulled the curtains, allowed her to keep her lights on, and went downstairs to see my guest off.

I then went upstairs again to find the hotel rocking with the ferocity of the storm, the wind whistling down the corridors and the lightning lighting up the lake.

Imogen was fast asleep.

I stood at my open window for a tiny space and Jill saw a ball of fire descend over Geneva. I watched the whole of the snowy Alps revealed momentarily as flash followed flash.

Then I went to bed and to sleep, only to be woken by almost deafening peals which caused me to pull the sheets over my head and turn on the light.

When I next woke the light was still on but the storm had passed.

Friday, 18th April, 1947

IF I wake at 3 a.m. I usually manage to get a fair slice of work done before the arrival of my morning tea, oddly called early, at seven. If I wake earlier I am apt to get tired before the first bird sings. If I wake later I am apt to rush things like a man allowing too little time for a train.

This morning the air was pleasantly cool after the night's storm. The gutters outside my window were wet but the streets below, when it became light enough for me to see them, were dry.

At 5.15 I looked out to see two curious dhows with very long thin crooked sail-masts go crazily across the lake wrapped in a spider-like embrace. I thought of my wife's suggestion that I should write a modern inverted *Hero and Leander* in which a lusty modern sports girl should swim the Lac Léman (appropriate to use the Montreux name for it here) to call on and, after a nocturnal embrace, to leave her T.B.-stricken lover. There would be a touch of Thomas Mann about that. I am strongly tempted to try it, but I should have to possess something of the astringent qualities of Somerset Maugham to tackle it satisfactorily.

But there's the germ of a good idea there. The girl would have, of course, to be a foreign agent, forbidden a passport to Switzerland. Hence her reason for swimming. I must listen to Imogen's reaction to this. Given the least encouragement she would set out to swim to the other side at 0° Centigrade without any such inducement as the thought of embracing any Leander on the further shore. She is not the sort of dog who needs a stick to be thrown into the water to induce her to swim.

The first bird to sing this morning began his song at 4.50. But I think he must have been a bad sleeper, because the chorus didn't really open till five. He sounded like a member of a B.B.C. symphony orchestra who had arrived too early for rehearsal. I expect he has been pecked to death.

When it was light enough to see I saw a veil of grey clouds above the Savoy Alps, and the summit of the Dent du Midi just below the clouds.

As the day drew clearer I noticed how much nearer the opposite hills had come. It now looked an easy distance to swim across. I wondered how many spies and refugees had achieved the feat in the war. It was the first time that I had been able to see as far as Lausanne which up to now had been hidden in a heat haze.

Jill woke as I turned on the light, told me several home truths about early risers including a statement that hardly bore looking into.

"I shall never sleep again," she said and turning over snored loudly.

We devoted the morning to finance, in other words the dispensing of money in the shops.

When I woke up I decided to give each of the children twenty francs to fritter away as they wished. It's hard to think of Lalage frittering away money in any currency, but I do want the children to get used to the decimal system.

As things are they find this ten notation just as obscure as our duodecimal notation.

After my usual comforting and solitary breakfast at seven I went into the lounge to work but was immediately disturbed by a Hoover. Of all the noises in the world I like that of the cleaner least. I associate it always with my father's last days in hospital.

I used to think that a dying man's last requests were apt to be granted, but not in an English hospital. Our so-called love of cleanliness is really a form of sadism.

I once wrote an article in praise of dust for *The Queen* which caused Jill to shun me for a whole day. She couldn't believe that I felt so strongly about being disturbed when I was in the throes of composition. I can't believe that this dusting business is anything but a form of jealousy. Women hate to see their menfolk interested in anything except them, and when I am writing I am interested only in that. When the mood is on there is nothing in the world I find so completely satisfying as writing. Love-making, skiing, and climbing mountains may take precedence in youth, but in old age physical ecstasy is supplanted by mental delight. "If youth but knew, if old age could but perform," is true only of the physical pleasures. True appreciation is an art learned only through years of experience.

I was talking about Hoovers. I left the lounge and went onto the terrace. It was too cold. I thought of having a second breakfast. I went for a short walk instead.

At nine o'clock we all set out for the shops. It was my intention first to call on the bank, but the family were all on edge to see if the second roll of films had come out or if, as my wife put it, I had again made a fool of myself. I hadn't. I looked down on thirty-six exquisitely clear interpretations of the Swiss scene. Little credit was due to me. I had a superb camera, and the light had been perfect. I had only to look through the viewfinder and press the button. My pride and pleasure were not shared by my family.

"I look a sight," said Jill. "I simply must do something about my weight."

"Why do you always take me in such awkward positions?" asked Lalage. "I never know when you're going to take us."

"You're not at Cheltenham now," I said. "You get no marks from me for deportment."

The charge for developing was only a franc, but the prints cost thirty-five francs more. I decided that my bank balance would not permit of many more photographs.

I then went on to the bank and the family settled down in a corner to quarrel over the photographs. Their passion for photographs is almost as fervid as their passion for films.

"Let me see," said Imogen. "You've seen that one twice. It isn't fair," and so on.

I elicited from the suave and ever polite cashier that whether you paid your hotel bill in advance in England or during your stay in Switzerland made no difference. The £75 allowed by a niggardly country had to cover that bill, but that £25 of that allocation might be spent in the shops.

He surveyed my authorisation forms much as an uncertain candidate might survey an unexpectedly difficult School Certificate paper. He decided that I might now have thirty francs in vouchers and 309 frs. 10 c. in cash, his exchange value for £20 less bank charge of 7 frs. 70 c. In all I had been able to obtain francs for £104 from this bank in addition to £40 worth of francs from my bank in Oxford after paying £120-odd at home for my journey and hotel expenses in advance. That is a total of £264 in all, or as I reckon £75 for myself, £75 for Jill, £75 for Lalage (aged fifteen) and £40 for Imogen (aged ten) and £1 tip for the bank.

I counted ruefully my remaining currency as I left the bank. I was reduced to 400 francs in vouchers and about 750 francs in cash. I had a week still to run of my fortnight and no serious shopping had yet been attempted. It looked as if I shouldn't be allowed to leave the country. I now saw the purpose of that £80 that I carried so carefully in an inner pocket.

"It is not," the cashier reminded me again sadly, "advisable to cash English notes. The rate of exchange is only 10 frs. 40 c."

I became angry at the thought of my country's lost prestige and felt that it was time to start another war.

In the meanwhile my family were anxious to begin their invasion of the shops.

"Have you got much money?" asked Lalage.

Foolishly I replied, "Enough to buy a crust."

It was at this moment that I tactlessly introduced my suggestion about the twenty francs.

"In future," I said, "I'm not buying your chocolates or postcards for you. You can buy your own. That'll teach you to count your change. Here's twenty francs each."

"I'm not taking twenty francs," said Lalage. "I'm not going to have you throwing your money about."

"Nor me," said Imogen. "Besides, I haven't got a purse."

"You little liar," said Lalage, "you've got at least three purses."

"I meant out here I haven't," said Imogen.

"Whose fault's that?" said Lalage.

I was taking up a considerable portion of the overcrowded bank's counter, but I was losing patience.

I emptied my pockets on to the counter.

"Count that," I said to Imogen.

She likes counting money.

"Now keep five francs," I said.

"I've nowhere to put it."

"I'll buy you a purse."

"You won't," said Lalage. "She's got too many already."

"You count," I said to her.

"I don't want to."

"You've damned well got to," I said. "I shall disinherit you if you don't."

Lalage obeyed. But her morning was completely ruined because entirely in order to please me she went off to shop and bought something (I don't know what) which was priced eighty-three centimes and the woman only gave her sixteen centimes change out of her franc.

"How much is a centime worth?" she kept on asking at too frequent intervals during the rest of the expedition.

"One-hundredth of 1s. 2d." I replied. "Call it 1s. 3d. One-hundredth of fifteen-pence. Can you work that out?"

She couldn't.

We went out of the bank to buy a purse for Imogen.

My luck seemed to be out. We turned over a hundred purses, one of which was a sort of deep well. I emptied my loose change into it and the assistant became almost English.

"I shan't be able to sell it now," she said. "It's soiled."

"I usually try on a hat before I buy one," I retorted. "I soil that much more. I oil my hair."

I'm not a good shopper.

Eventually Imogen decided on an absurd thing shaped like a heart in blue and scarlet leather. As I was pretty sure that she would lose it before the day was out I made no demur.

I pulled Jill away with difficulty from some earrings and we went in search of shoes for Lalage. She had, I gathered, a sudden desire to be grown-up and would only have what I call co-respondent's shoes. I left them wrangling in a sea of shoes and went out into the market-place which was gay and colourful.

The booths were crowded with women carrying string-bags bulging with oranges, lemons, carrots and cabbages. I was attracted by a voluble man dressed as a chef in white cap and apron who was performing miracles with deft fingers and a shining galvanised aluminium slicer.

He spoke slowly and with the air of a distinguished critic as he sliced potatoes into wafer-like disks and shredded cabbages and carrots into long curling fingers.

"*Manger froid*," I heard him say.

"*C'est exquis*," he added, holding his instrument high in the air and taking it skilfully to pieces and enumerating the virtues of each part like an infatuated sergeant explaining the parts of the rifle to particularly dumb recruits.

I watched him entranced. So did a couple of hundred other sightseers who included a grizzled peasant in dirty light blue boiler-suit and age-old skiing cap, a lovely young girl with long hair of burnished copper, a sober-looking citizen in sombre black

1 NEAR VILLARS

2 IMOGEN TAKES A SUN-BATH

3 ROMANCE ABOVE THE LAKE

4 THE SWAN LAKE

5 IMOGEN ON THE PIER

7 THE CASTLE OF CHILLON

9 MILK-SHAKE TIME

11 GARDEN OF REMEMBRANCE

12 BELOW THE BASTION

13 VINEYARDS, TERRITET

14 FRENCH WAR MEMORIAL 1914–8

15 LOOKING OUT ON CLARENS

16 VILLENEUVE

17 GSTAAD : THE WASSERNGRAT

18 GSTADD : SKI LIFT

19 IMOGEN ON TOP OF THE WORLD

21 RHONE VALLEY AND LAKE OF GENEVA

22 EASTERN END OF THE LAKE OF GENEVA

23 NEAR VILLARS

25 MAIN STREET, VILLARS

27 GRINDELWALD AND THE WETTERHORN

28 MATTERHORN AND THE LAKE OF RIFFEL

29 LANGWIES VIADUCT, NEAR AROSA

30 JUNGFRAU FROM INTERLAKEN

31 LAUTERBRUNNEN

33 SPRING FLOWERS

34 DENT DU MIDI

35 GOTHARD ROAD NEAR THE DEVIL'S BRIDGE

37 WILD CROCUSES

38 RHONE VALLEY

39 COL DES MOSSES

41 LA GRUYÈRE CHURCH

43 WEDDING AT LA GRUYÈRE

44 CHATEAU D'OEX

45 THE BLUE LAKE NEAR KANDERSTAG

46 CHAMPERY

47 STATUES AT GENEVA

48 BERNE

and buxom farmwomen in from the country. I felt a tug at my elbow.

I looked down to see Imogen.

"You're wanted," she said.

I went back to the shoe-shop to find Lalage and Jill entirely surrounded by a sea of shoes.

"There's nothing here," said Lalage.

"I think there's something wrong with my eyes," I said.

I led them out into the market-place.

In a moment Jill too was under the thrall of the slicer seller. She had no need to tell me.

I elbowed my way through the crowd. The vendor allowed for no interruption until he had completed his act which took the greater part of a quarter of an hour. I knew that he was drawing near the fall of the curtain because he selected a small boy out of the gaping crowd and instead of telling him to run away as an Englishman would have done he put the instrument in his hands and made him work it. The child, suddenly drawn out of the audience on to the stage, blushed to the roots of his hair, but even under his clumsy hands the thing worked. We were convinced. There was a mad rush forward and paper money was dangled under the nose of the chef with all the eagerness with which money on racecourses is pushed into the hands of bookies.

"*Neuf francs*," I heard the man say and I pushed two five-franc notes into his hand. In exchange I got to my surprise two slicers wrapped in newspaper.

I said the first thing that came into my head.

"*Complet?*" I asked.

"*Mais oui, m'sieu, complet,*" he said and served the next customer.

"Why on earth," said Lalage, "did you get two?"

For once my brain functioned.

"For G," I said. "A present for G. G'll love it."

G is a neighbouring housewife with a passion for gadgets.

"You think of everything," said Jill admiringly.

I looked up to find that I was being photographed by an American soldier as a typical Swiss farmer having a day out in Montreux. Have I told you that I always wear a skiing cap?

We continued our search for shoes for Lalage. On the way I passed an antique shop.

"I want an old coloured print of Chillon," I said.

Lalage immediately became reproving.

"The way you waste money," she said and walked on ahead.

"We've got three hundred and fifty-seven pictures for which there's no room on the walls," said Jill.

"This'll make an even number," I said. "I like even numbers."

The antique dealer turned out the contents of five deep drawers. I left him to it and went on to a tobacconist's.

"Twenty-five Partagas," I said.

"At 1 fr. 75 c.?" he said.

"Just that," I said and went out encumbered with a box much too large to hide from Lalage.

"What have you been buying now?" she asked surveying the box with great disfavour.

"I'm looking for a pair of shoes for you."

We passed a very small and insignificant-looking cobbler's shop nearly opposite the station.

"You go in there and rest," I said. "I've got to get some refills for my notebook."

"Why?" asked Lalage.

"Because if I haven't a notebook we starve."

"You know you love buying notebooks," said Jill.

"I said refills," I said. "Come on, Imogen."

Imogen and I passed a heavenly quarter of an hour turning over leather-bound notebooks. As neither Lalage nor Jill was present I became quite reckless.

"You must get the note-taking habit early," I said. "Here's a beauty."

Imogen agreed and took out her heart-shaped purse.

"No," I said, "this is on me."

"Then why give me money to buy my own things?" asked my practical-minded daughter.

"That's for the stomach," I said.

"Choose the one you want. I'm taking this one," I added.

"But, Daddy, you've got heaps and heaps of notebooks," she said.

"Not a Swiss one," I said, as I lovingly smelt the blue leather.

We went back to the shoe-shop to find Lalage strutting up and down in an extremely attractive pair of solid brown leather walking-shoes.

"Now, they're something like," I said.

"Something like what?" asked Imogen.

"Something like shoes," I added and turned to the assistant. "*Combien?*" I asked.

Those shoes cost me 59 frs. 50 c. with tax.

In spite of her protests I could see how desperately Lalage wanted them.

It was now Jill's turn. Luckily she couldn't get into any frock that she tried on. With our arms almost breaking under parcels we emerged into the open air.

"I want a drink," I said.

We sat in the sun outside the Metropole and I took photographs of Imogen testing the temperature of the lake while the waitress went off in search of Campari and milk-shakes. It had been a profitable morning.

We took an early tram home and found it overcrowded with sojourners from Poona. The Poonaites are always in time for luncheon, and luncheon in Switzerland is at 12.30.

At two o'clock we were at the station where I forgot as usual to present a voucher for my railway ticket.

We boarded the Zweisimmen train for Les Avants. The single fare was 2 frs. 90 c.

At 2.8 we began the smooth climb out of Montreux up through a land of white cherry-blossom and bare vineyards, past the square castle of Blonay. I went to sleep to wake up in a country of green fields and hedgeless roads, of steep ravines and dense pine-woods high above the still lake on which half a dozen boats were lying idle as painted boats upon a painted ocean. We turned and twisted up the mountain-side and arrived at 2.40 at Les Avants, which seems to consist entirely of a funicular and the vast girls' school of Châtelard.

A thick-set grizzled man in a boiler-suit and climbing-boots carrying an alpenstock pointed to the left and said "*Gauche*" when I asked him the way to Glion, and we began our first walk in Switzerland.

The track was a rough mountain road which descended steeply through a wood carpeted with myriads of wild flowers. Imogen's new notebook quickly became a bed of violets, anemonies, cowslips, and flowers of which I didn't know the names. We met no one for three miles except a woodcutter, a woodman, a farmer and a man pushing a bicycle. All four of them greeted us as old friends.

We rested on a bridge over a gorge and threw banana-skins into the flowing torrent to have an Oxford and Cambridge boat race. Cambridge won every time.

We looked up at the bare rock of Jarman standing six thousand feet above.

When we were halfway down Lalage suddenly discovered that she had left her new sun-glasses somewhere. She looked as distressed as if she were about to have a major operation. First she thought she had left them in the train. I tried to reassure her that if that were so we should quickly reclaim them in a country as honest as Switzerland.

Then she thought that she had left them just outside Les Avants station where we had sat down to enjoy the view. I left Imogen and Jill to saunter quietly on while Lalage and I climbed back up the long hill.

The woodcutter seemed surprised to see us. I couldn't say "*Bon jour, m'sieu*," again. I tried a variant.

"*Très chaud*," I said.

"*Très chaud*," he repeated.

But neither he nor I knew whether I was referring to us, him or the day.

"I feel such a fool," said Lalage, "continually passing and repassing him. What shall we say when we go back?"

"'I've found my glasses' or 'I've lost my glasses,'" I said. "What's the French for 'glasses'?"

"I've no idea."

"What do I pay for at Cheltenham?" I said.

We found her glasses, and on the way down Lalage made me give her a test on *Macbeth* which she is taking in School Certificate. I tried to bring my mind back from the mossy flower-covered banks, the glimpses of the Savoy Alps seen through the pines, the cascading waters below, and the black gigantic sentinel rock of Jarman above. But the appeal of nature was too strong. I really at the moment couldn't care less whether Macbeth couldn't sleep or Lady Macbeth couldn't help walking and saying things in her sleep.

When we caught up with Jill and Imogen they were marooned high above us in a cleft of a tree and couldn't move up or down.

I laughed happily and sat on a bank and looked thousands of feet down at the lake.

"You can jump or roll for all I care," I said.

"We waited for you," said Imogen.

"And now I'm waiting for you," I said.

Hours later we came to Glion, and resisted the temptation to feed at the first half-dozen restaurants that advertised VUE SPLENDIDE. It was a *vue splendide* all right.

We looked two thousand feet down on the lake and up the broad Rhône valley to the Dent du Midi. Eventually we entered the garden of a tea-room immediately above the station. It was filled with English people, and it was only after I had ordered our *thé complet* that I realised that we had come to the wrong place. Another hundred yards and we should have been lying in deck chairs under the shade of the trees in the exquisite garden of the vast white mansion known as the Grand Hôtel Righi Vaudois.

One gets so accustomed in England to sink with delight into any place that offers refreshment that I had forgotten momentarily that in Switzerland food and drink are obtainable at almost every halting-place. That helps to make it the ideal walkers' country.

Some day I propose to have a meal at the Grand Hôtel Righi Vaudois to make up for the relatively poor tea supplied in the tea-rooms. We had stale toasted rolls and plum jelly. It cost eight francs for the four of us. We were paying for the view and that, but not the tea, was cheap at the price.

I suspect that we should have had cherry jam if we had stopped at the Café des Narcisses on the outskirts of Glion, but I was put off that by the sight of a small boy just below squirting liquid manure through a long hose-pipe much too generously on a single grass patch that he was rapidly turning into a cesspool.

From the tea-rooms (by the way, always avoid tea-rooms. They always attract the English!) I looked down over the station and the funicular to the lake, and left-handed on the other side of a field cut by an attractive path under cherrry trees I saw a church perched on the edge of a rock with a covered cloister that looked out on the Rhône valley and across to the Savoy Alps.

I became impatient because Jill would keep on calling the place

Val-Mai, on the strength of a large poster on the station platform which bore that name.

"It must be the name of the station," she said. "There's no other."

"You might with equal reason call every station in France Byrrh," I said. "It's an advertisement for a clinic and says so if you can read."

The children told me not to be so rude and cruel to their darling mother and I got up in a fury and started walking over the field-path towards the church. I had meant to take their photographs crossing the field but I suddenly wanted to be alone. I had wanted to give them a good tea and foolishly chosen the wrong place.

There is something about a field-path that always attracts me. Perhaps it is because of their rapid disappearance in England.

The church was locked and I wondered why it was that only the Catholics regard prayer as part of the normal routine of life.

I recovered my lost equanimity in the cloisters, for all the views were stupendous and vastly enhanced by being framed in the arches. The family caught me up and I took the opportunity to use those arches as a frame to take their photographs.

There were several alternative ways down but I chose the forward track past a lot of models of chalets. This track was sign-posted MONT FLEURI. I came to a junction where four ways met and shouted to some boys playing in the steep wood below. They shouted back "Oui! Oui!" They would, I felt, have said, "Oui! Oui!" if I had said "Piccadilly Circus."

I took the track that left Mont Fleuri funicular station on my right, crossed a road, entered and passed through the entrance to a large house and on the further side found a narrow steep track. "*Très zigzag*," said Imogen.

I looked down through the trees to a deep ravine at the bottom of which rose a white, sunny and happy-looking cemetery.

I started zigzagging and at the cemetery found a signpost pointing up the way I had come. MONT FLEURI 1 KM. I read. VAL-MONT 2 KM. GLION 3 KM.

It seemed a short two miles. I cut through the cemetery to take a track passing its high wall on which were growing flowers that I couldn't place.

I looked down on the roof of the Bonivard.

At the foot of this track I loitered on a bridge bearing the date 1693 and looked at the terra-cotta walls of the Local des Pompes on one side and Maison de Commune 1768 on the other.

I was in a medieval suburb of Montreux. Vatana perhaps. It consisted of a very narrow street with tall houses under each of which deep cellars had been constructed for the wine. A girl sat in the shade of one of these knitting. In another a man was sawing wood.

At the end of the street the lane descended steeply to the bottom of the high rock that abuts on the main lake shore road and I passed the house where the ammunition is stored on the ground floor and within a minute was literally in the arms of the enchanting waitress at the Taverne du Château de Chillon, for she saw me coming and ran with outstretched arms to greet me with a smile.

A little old man trailing a yellow go-cart full of boughs came in for perhaps a châteaubriand or a blue trout and I settled down in the sun with Hilda.

I had discovered that her name was Hilda because she wore a brooch of silver bearing the letter H, and on my inquiring said, "Eelda."

At seven o'clock I was up in my hotel bedroom watching the golden sun rush much too quickly behind the western hills. All too quickly the glowing golden path over the lake vanished, leaving a rose-pink tint in the sky which was reflected in the opalescent lake.

One part of the lake was now pearl-grey. The base of the Savoy Alps was black, the top of the Dent du Midi pale as a ghost. Thin blue haze hung over the Rhône valley and a thin veil of light grey hung over Montreux. It was a perfect night.

After dinner, at which we drank Neuchâtel at 6 frs. 50 c., I took the family in to see a French film called *Les Ailles Blanches*. We went down to the tram-stop at 8.10. No tram appeared till 8.30. It was cold now that the sun had set, and in my hurry I had forgotten to bring a coat.

If there is one thing in life that I dread more than another it is catching cold, and I catch cold easily. I paced up and down, cursing and fuming. Lunn's man chose that moment to present me with the account for the Champéry trip. It came to 47 frs. 70 c., which struck me as far too much. I was angry about that.

When we got to the cinema at 8.50 the woman at the office refused to accept my vouchers.

This held up the queue for a long time at which I was pleased, but when I got inside I found the place almost deserted and the news still on.

There was a good reel of the England v. France Rugger match at which the Swiss laughed immoderately.

Then came the film. I couldn't understand more than an odd word. The cinema was cold. I was cold. I endured such agony that I couldn't even sleep. I tried to follow the captions which were in German.

The story appeared to be about a gay composer who was also a convent organist. He had two gay daughters who danced in revue and a very serious one who had to confess to her father that she was an expectant but unmarried mother. That appears to be a thing that French fathers get hysterical about.

There was a sub-plot in which a girl of no particular attraction got herself engaged to an enormously wealthy young man, but when his father went broke she seized the occasion to hand her lover back his ring and go into a nunnery, which she would have been well advised to do at the start as God had not endowed her with any sex-appeal.

Here again the French seem to me to go wildly wrong. If one of two rich partners loses a fortune surely there's enough left for the two to live comfortably on the more than adequate income of the one who didn't go broke.

I was glad to see the grave of the rich man. He died young, so God must have loved him. I found him commonplace. Indeed I found the whole show commonplace and even turgid.

I want to see no more French films of that calibre. The family, however, united in describing it as "wizard."

My fury which had been threatening to erupt like Etna ever since tea burst at the *entr'acte* when I announced that I was going home.

"You can't desert us here," said my wife putting on the injured voice of a heroine abandoned among a horde of dervishes.

"I'm cold," I said. "I think I'm going to have pneumonia."

"You always think you're going to have pneumonia."

"I've had it twice. The third time may not be lucky."

I decided to console myself and the children with sweets.

I bought a bar of chocolate.

Lalage was livid.

"Honestly, Daddy," she said.

I called the man back and went within an ace of buying his whole consignment.

There are moments when I feel that I am not after all quite the perfect father.

The lights went down. I settled down to endure a few hours' more agony.

When the silly affair was over I refused to speak. I walked up and down the deserted streets waiting for a tram. When it arrived I started playing Rugger with the other passengers.

On arrival at the hotel I went up to bed without a word.

I did just chuck Imogen under the chin, but even that gesture was misunderstood. She thought I was trying to hit her.

Saturday, 19th April, 1947

THE first bird mistook the time. He started his chant at 4.30. When his still sleeping neighbours had dealt with him there was silence till five o'clock.

As I walked up and down in the sun in the early morning I watched a large number of jeeps go past containing Swiss soldiers with guns. I was first struck by their extreme youthfulness, then by their good health and then by their seriousness. These boys all seemed to be sitting at attention, holding their rifles upright, looking straight ahead, and not even speaking. They had all the seriousness of children playing a game. They looked like public-school girls practising deportment.

I was glad to see them pass because I like my lake to myself in the early morning and I usually get it. Looking across the water at the Savoy Alps and the Dent du Midi is an occupation of which I do not easily tire, but people distract me from it.

Another early riser buttonholed me on the terrace and asked where she could find a book on Byron and Shelley in the Alps.

"I don't think," I said "that Shelley left much impression on the lakeside people. It was Byron who swept all Europe off its feet."

"Dislikable men both," she said.

"I wouldn't mind being detestable if I could write as they wrote," I replied.

"I'm sure you wouldn't behave to women as they behaved," she said archly.

I didn't like the way the conversation was going.

"There are times," I said, "when my wife has accused me of behaving worse than either of them."

An enchanting young girl with short, flounced scarlet frock, white blouse and glorious glistening hair passed below on a bicycle singing a sweet Swiss air softly to herself. I know her well. She often passes the Taverne as I drink, and invariably smiles.

Byron I felt would have felt very much at home with her. She was too a type who would have appealed to Shelley. I wanted to get rid of the Englishwoman.

"You are of course an ardent admirer of the work of both poets," I said.

"Shelley," she replied sternly, "was an atheist. Byron was too facile."

That was just a little more than I could stand from a forbidding countryman who was distracting my attention from the Swiss miss.

"Shelley worshipped beauty. We worship ugliness," I retorted. "Our present-day poets are unmelodious and unintelligible. *Don Juan* is facile exactly as *Hamlet* was facile. It is the facility of genius. I wish I had it."

"I had no idea that anybody really read either poet these days for pleasure."

"It's our loss if we don't," I said, and walked away.

I wish I had the poet's gift for expressing the profound impression made on my emotions by the hills and the lake or by the black-haired slender-legged young girls who were continually delighting my eye.

Removed from the disapproving eyes of Lalage, Jill, Imogen and I spent a riotously extravagant morning in the shops.

My turn came first. I achieved a huge volume that weighed

about a hundredweight, and contained several hundred full-page plates, many of them coloured, on the Alps. It was a superbly produced book and cost me thirty-two francs.

That set the pace for the morning.

I next bought a leather-bound notebook with six refills for Imogen and a leather-bound notebook with six refills for myself. I had filled one notebook of my own and was unable to buy refills for it.

I then bought a hundred-year-old coloured print of Chillon with the Dent du Midi in the background for ten francs and decided that it was Jill's turn.

We entered a sports shop where she bought a thick off-white woollen skiing sweater of a type that I have seen many Swiss girls wearing. This cost eighty-six francs. She then bought an old-fashioned skiing cap of dark blue cloth for ten francs, and Imogen, after a good deal of protestation, allowed herself to accept a round soft chamois-skin bag which was decorated with the figure of a black silky young chamois. This cost thirty francs. Jill then fell for a pair of very soft co-respondent's shoes (white and brown) which to my surprise became her well.

After we had ransacked about fifteen shops I discovered that I had lost my new diary. We retraced our steps and revisited about six of them. In each of them the assistant thought that I was anxious to buy something. It is difficult enough for a non-French-speaking Englishman to make his wants understood. It is infinitely more difficult trying to make his losses understood. In the end I fell back on saying, "*J'oubliais*," and then describing a notebook by gesture. I elicited a vast amount of sympathy but very little understanding. Most of the shopkeepers thought that I had mislaid Lalage or a dog.

Jill then discovered that she had been carrying the lost diary in her handbag for safety. I felt in need of a drink. We settled down outside the Metropole, and I watched three boys idly fishing from the pier and five stalwart business-like English girls devoid of any physical attraction go past weighed down with over-heavy rucksacks and the same grim expression that has since the war been the Englishman's eternal mask.

For once we arrived back at the hotel before the gong had sounded for luncheon. I left Jill and Imogen to make their peace with Lalage and walked quickly off to the Taverne for a drink and a brief chat (if you could call it that when neither understands the other's words) with the adorable Hilda.

At luncheon, after ordering for myself a bottle of Johannesburg Ravanay at six francs, I suddenly discovered an apple-juice called Ranseier which helped to make Lalage view our extravagances in a more mellow light. I was called to the telephone to find that Lunn's man had failed to book seats for us for Villars, so we were thrown back on our own devices. I decided to take the family to Lausanne.

"That means," said Lalage wearily, "more shops."

"That's quite right," I said, forgetting my vow. I wondered how the Cambridge farmer was getting on at Lugano.

At 2.33 we caught a slow train (omnibus) from Territet. The return fare was 2 frs. 90 c. each. I spent the journey standing at the open carriage window looking out over the lake along the shores of which the track for the most part ran. Not altogether at the lake. At Montreux station we were joined by a very smartly dressed girl in grey coat and skirt, grey round pillbox-shaped hat, silk stockings (of course) and very high-heeled shoes which showed her beauty to great advantage.

At Clarens we took aboard several wooden boxes packed tight with deep blue pansies, a deep bell boomed, a porter waved a disk of green and white as if he were a marker on a shooting-range, and we glided on.

At Burier I noticed that vineyards were being cultivated right up to the station door and that a big white house on a knoll had an avenue of cypresses.

At La Tour de Peilz we took aboard more boxes of yellow pansies and several milk-churns. Imogen was entranced by the sight of lizards flashing past in the sun.

At Vevey we were reminded by the crowds that it was Saturday afternoon.

From then on we ran alongside the beach, and Imogen nearly fell out of the window craning her neck to see a small child who was paddling.

"Goody, goody," she said. "They'll be bathing soon."

But along the whole twenty miles of shore we saw no sign of a bather in spite of the blue sky and summer heat.

At Epesses, a quite tiny hamlet, we were joined by a bevy of lovely young girls all dressed most becomingly and smartly.

These girls all wore their frocks as if they had put them on for the first time that morning.

At Villette (did Charlotte Brontë get her title from this suburb of Lausanne?) Jill decided that she wanted to settle for life in one of the enchanting villas that bordered the water-front.

At Lutry we were joined by a twelve-year-old girl who boarded the train quite casually as it was moving.

At Pelly village I noticed that the porter was wearing a gold wrist-watch. Hilda carries a silver pencil, buys her very smart shoes in Lausanne, and wears stockings of the finest silk, and here was a porter wearing a gold wrist-watch. This seemed to me democracy in the working. England is a land where we are for ever conscious of class distinctions. In Switzerland there appears to be neither aristocracy nor pauper. Every man calls every other man " m'sieu," every man raises his hat to his fellows, irrespective of sex, everybody shakes hands on meeting. The Swiss are as instinctively good-mannered as we are ill-mannered.

The streets of Lausanne are at least as crowded as Oxford Street, but I saw no sign of jostling.

Everybody had time both to look in the entrancing shop-windows and to make room for his neighbour.

On leaving the vast station, which is made brighter by many show-cases of jewellery, shoes, and other objects of delight, we climbed up a narrow cobbled street, quite as steep as the street of Clovelly, to the main centre where stand in close proximity the enormous Lausanne Palace Hotel, the palace of glass known as the post-office, and the red-roofed cathedral.

On the way up I noticed that all the girls were dressed most becomingly and all had very shapely legs.

" If that's what hill-climbing does I must try it," said Jill.

" It isn't your legs that need reducing," said Lalage with the true candour of a daughter.

Imogen gazed longingly at a street-vendor painting balloons and blowing rainbow-coloured bubbles. I gazed longingly at a calf-skin attaché case with brass locks priced at two hundred francs and at a Rolex Oyster watch that never needed winding up. Jill gazed longingly at frocks and shoes and Lalage walked with her head in the air indifferent to temptations that beset the rest of us. Imogen found an escalator going up into an arcade and blocked the traffic by insisting on trying to walk down it.

I looked up at a crowd of drinkers sitting on an open balcony above the square. Imogen spotted the words OLD INDIA—DANCING and we went up some narrow stairs and found ourselves in a pillared hall with a view over the lake to the Savoy Alps.

I sat down and took up the menu.

Every variety of whisky was apparently obtainable at six francs a time. I decided to be parsimonious.

For myself I ordered Russian tea, for Jill coffee, for Lalage a coffee ice, for Imogen a strawberry ice. We resisted the temptation to try the pâtisserie. In other words we ate nothing. The bill came to 8 frs. 50 c. or just about ten shillings. The waiter had the grace to give me back my franc tip. "Service," he said, "is included." Can you imagine an English waiter doing that?

We arrived there at four. It was practically empty. The orchestra struck up at 4.30. The crooner was an English girl. By five o'clock it was crowded. Young girls came in unattended. An English mother arrived with two small children. A number of youths of the type that one always associates with dancing sat down and ordered short drinks.

Everybody appeared to have money to burn. Everybody was extremely well dressed.

We went off to explore the medieval cathedral. I found it almost as bare a building as Geneva. The woodwork of the seats, which were solid, was the best thing about it; the Bible was read from a heavy table. Seats occupied the position usually taken by the altar. There was some repulsive stained glass. There was no place to kneel down. There was no one about and I wasn't surprised. It was a relief to leave so barren a place. We went on climbing (in Lausanne there is only uphill) and looking into shops, sweet-shops, pâtisseries, papeteries, leather-shops, clothes-shops, watch-shops, all displaying goods of great delicacy of design, all very highly priced.

But I was less interested in the shops than in the people. There is no getting away from the fact that the girls of Lausanne are remarkably comely, and I did not want to get away from it. I am always cheered up by the presence of lovely women. They stepped lightly as chamois up these precipitous thoroughfares in spite of their high-heeled shoes.

At 5.15 several of the shops were already shut in spite of its being Saturday.

At six o'clock we joined the downhill rush to the station. At 6.5 precisely our train left. In our compartment were a crowd of noisy exhibitionist boys who kept up a fierce running commentary until they mercifully left us at Vevey. I saw nothing notable on the return journey except two black-headed gulls standing by the lakeside and a steamer moored up at Rivez.

I was glad when we drew nearer to the mountains that overhang Montreux. I was equally glad when we left the train at Chillon and climbed up to the Taverne to tell Hilda of our afternoon adventure.

After dinner I took the family to see Rita Hayworth in *Tonight and Every Night*. There was a long queue at the box-office. Obviously Switzerland, like England, goes gay on Saturday nights.

I was delighted with the film. I had never before seen Rita Hayworth, or even wanted to. I found that she not only has considerable charm, but is natural. She not only looks good, she also acts well. The story which is done in admirable technicolor is negligible, the dancing is of its kind perfect. England beats the world at telling a story on the films. America is unbeatable at musicals. I came out mightily refreshed. For once I was able to agree with the family that it was " wizard."

Sunday, 20th April, 1947

At 4.40 this morning a bumble-bee in the curtains woke up and mistook my light for daylight. He might have suffered more. Within a minute the first bird burst into song, but both the bumble-bee and the bird had been forestalled by a man who passed below my window at 4.30 whistling. He was whistling in the rain. I had come to regard rain as a thing of the past. I had forgotten its sound. I found it pleasant. I looked out at dawn to see the mountain tops wreathed in mist. The rain was falling so gently that I couldn't believe it until I went out of doors to test it. It had the English property of being wet. I borrowed two umbrellas and set off with my family for High Mass at the Catholic church at ten o'clock. I had great difficulty in finding it, and on arrival found my way barred outside the main doors by lottery-ticket sellers, an excellent idea in a country where people go to church, but not so profitable in England, where they don't.

It was a large church, but we found it crowded to capacity when we got inside. I am always at a disadvantage in a crowded church and invariably go for the wrong seat. I wanted the children to see the pageantry, but the main aisle was filled. I elected to occupy the front seat of a side-aisle from which place we could see what was happening to the right of the altar but little else. This upset Lalage, who dislikes attracting attention.

It was only when I had taken up my position that Lalage angrily pointed to the gallery where there were many empty seats. She regards it as blasphemy to speak in the House of God, but she pointed, and the expression on her face was like that on the face of one's captain when one has dropped the pass that would have meant a certain try and victory. Jill then saw a vacant seat in the front row of the main asle. She made as if to go. I noticed that it was covered with red carpet.

"I shouldn't," I said. "You never know. The actors may want it."

Perhaps, as you may be reading this inattentively, I had better explain that we are not Catholics. We are properly brought up members of the Church of England. That is to say, we seldom go to church, except to Holy Communion at Easter. As I am by nature a natural worshipper of God and talk to Him quite a lot that may seem odd. The reason is that I don't like the sort of people I see in church. They are even grimmer than the rest of us and dress even more appallingly.

I believe that God likes us either not to worship communally or to put a little colour into it. I cannot believe that I should ever gain any spiritual consolation or exultation from attending the bare cathedrals of Lausanne or Geneva, and I certainly should find it less easy to thank God for His blessings there than in an Alpine meadow covered with gentian and edelweiss.

I wasn't surprised to see this Catholic church crowded. In the first place it is a place of great beauty. There were images of the Blessed Virgin, of shining angels or archangels with glorious wings, and of all sorts of saints. There was a moving effigy of Christ on the Cross. I liked the splendour of the priests' robes, though I think the biretta has an incongruous touch about it.

I like immensely the Plain-song. ("Just like the African negroes' incantations, isn't it?" said Jill rather too loudly. It disturbed Lalage in her prayers. She was kneeling most uncomfortably, bolt upright.)

I said to Imogen,

" It's quite easy to follow. It's only the Communion Service in Latin or it may be French."

To which she replied,

" What's Communion, Daddy?"

I don't in the least mind talking in church, but I felt that the question called for notice. The mystic rite is not so simple as all that.

" The priest is changing the bread and water into flesh and blood," I said.

" Is that why the people keep bobbing up and down?" she asked.

Without waiting for my answer she began genuflecting as nearly in time with the rest of the congregation as she could.

She was getting a lot of fun out of it.

She especially liked the Sanctus.

" What's that?"

" Bells to remind the sleepy ones who think they're praying that the deed is consummated."

" I wish you'd talk sense, Daddy."

" Go on bobbing," I said. " You look just like a dipper."

A priest in very short scarlet surplice climbed the pulpit and began announcing coming events in turn with a second announcer who stood below in the chancel.

He then lowered his voice and became slightly, but only slightly, parsonic.

" This is the sermon," I said.

" I know that," said Imogen and gazed upward at an angle of eighty-three degrees. I felt that she was about to have quite a pain in the neck.

The priest spoke simply, with scarcely any gesticulation, and without any notes. He spoke for perhaps a quarter of an hour, without a single pause or a single " er."

He kept on repeating the phrase, " le bon pasteur."

" It's all about the Good Shepherd," I said.

" I know that," said Imogen. " Don't interrupt. I want to listen."

The sermon over we had a collection. I handed down the pew

three five-centime bits. Lalage returned mine with a frown. The collection was taken by men. There is nothing remarkable about that. But a second collection was taken later on by women and I was unprepared for that. I passed three farthings down the pew.

The woman collector said, "*Merc'*" for each separate offering. I felt mean. Churchwardens in England never say thank you. I felt at a grave disadvantage coming from so impolite a race.

The organ burst into a cheerful roar.

"It's all over," I said to Lalage. "You needn't kneel any more."

On the way out we were again besieged by sellers of lottery tickets. The transition from the spiritual to the material seemed abrupt.

Lalage without a word walked away in front of us, obviously worried.

She is much more deeply religious than I am. She was shocked because of my whisperings.

"I'll go and look after her," said Imogen, who is the most deeply religious of any of us.

"We're going to look for a bathing-place," I lied.

We walked down in the wake of the congregation and I noticed that a large proportion of them were smartly dressed attractive young girls. Smartly dressed attractive girls don't often attend the Established Church of England services at home.

The sun was now out. The flower-beds in the public gardens were filled with multi-coloured tulips. The quai walk was crowded with laughing, colourful youth. Men were playing tennis. Spring was in the air. I wanted to sing.

"I'm going to call on Hilda," I said.

An elderly English couple with sad drawn faces came towards us. They looked very Poona.

"I thought the pews were unnecessarily hard," said the man.

They had obviously been to a service in the English church.

We found Lalage sitting on a seat overlooking the lake with her head bowed in her hands.

She looked as if she were still praying.

"Don't disturb her," said Jill.

" Knees hurting?" I said.

" Like hell," said Lalage.

" I thought the pews were unnecessarily hard," I said.

" You thought nothing of the sort. You adored it. But you shouldn't talk in church."

"You're quite right," I said, forgetting again.

" If you adore it so why don't you become a Catholic?"

" Because I don't like being ordered about by priests. I must be free. But it's an older form of religion than ours. You ought to read Macaulay."

She looked at me, startled.

" I'm trying to do a bit of Macaulay now for précis. I can't make head or tail of it."

" Give me the book."

She handed it to me.

This was one of those amazing coincidences that could only happen in real life.

The passage was the one I had been thinking of.

" I'll tell you what it's about. The age of the Catholic Church. He says it's very old."

" Is that all? Why take so long over it?"

" That was Macaulay's way. Like the Catholics, he likes a bit of colour."

She stopped in front of a tennis court.

" I'm staying here."

" Very wise of you," I said, and passed on.

We came to a little jutting-out piece of rock occupied by a woman, three men and two children.

They were all fishing.

As we watched the woman caught a silver-looking tiny fish.

Removing it from the hook she gouged its eyes out.

" I don't think the Swiss love animals," said Jill, " only a sprinkling of dogs, and look what they do to fish."

I was looking out over the lake at a man in a sailing dhow shouting at the perambulators on the quai.

" How would you like to sail to Chillon?" I said.

Nobody was listening. Imogen was lost in pity for the poor fish.

Jill was admiring the graceful carriage of the passing cavalcade of churchgoers.

I walked on looking out over the Savoy mountains from under the shade of weeping willows.

The beauty was almost too much for me.

"I'm frightfully hot," said Jill, "I'm going up to the hotel to take off some clothes."

"I'll take them up for you," I said.

"I can't undress here," she said.

"I don't see why not," I said. "We do at Brighton."

"Montreux's not Brighton. Look at that notice."

I read BAINS INTERDIT.

"I think it's a pity," I said, "that Calvin was ever born."

"I don't see the connexion."

"He put ideas into people's heads."

"Eve ate the apple before Calvin."

"Calvin came to remind us of that."

We walked up by the side of a mountain torrent towards the hotel and I, longing for Hilda and Campari, refused to wait.

About halfway I heard the distant voice of Imogen.

"Daddy, Daddy," she cried.

Imogen has never called to me in vain.

She came running, all legs and arms and smiles, and took my hand in her small hot one.

We spent the remainder of the morning taking photographs of Chillon in the intervals of drinking.

The owner of the Taverne came out to talk.

"I have only bought this place since October. I give it to my son. It is a good place. This is one of the main roads in Switzerland. It is the main road to the St. Bernard, the main road to the Simplon, the main road to Lucerne. But I do not like the rise in prices. We give a hundred thousand francs for a small chalet and a thousand francs a month to a workman. Double what we gave before the war."

No wonder, I thought, that porters wear gold wrist-watches and Hilda carries a silver pencil and an expensive streamline fountain-pen if they and she get sixty pounds a month.

While I was watching the arrival of American G.I.s on leave from Germany with their attractive girl-friends, Indians and Chilians and the rest, Jill suddenly gave a cry of delight.

"A swallow," she said. "You owe me five bob."

It was indeed a swallow.

"Why did that fool say that they didn't get here till June?"

"Nobody ever knows anything about birds," said Jill. "You ought to have realised that by this time."

We got up to take some more photographs and then sauntered home a quarter of an hour late for luncheon. We drank a bottle of Burle Fer Johannesberg at six francs. It was extremely good.

In response to Imogen's importunity we set off after luncheon armed with bathing-suits by train for Villeneuve, the Montreux Plage. The only other place where bathers are allowed to undress and bathe in the lake is just below the Bonivard, but the Swiss have not the bathing habit. We found the Plage completely abandoned. The whole world on the other hand was drinking at tables under the trees.

I made for a tower which I mistook for a church only to find that it was the police station. I sauntered out onto the pierhead and watched small boys fishing until the white steamer drew in, as overcrowded as it had been on the previous Sunday.

We watched the s.s. *Vevey* pull out for Lausanne and Geneva and were not surprised at her emptiness. There was nothing in those towns to attract Sunday afternoon visitors in a heat-wave; on the other hand the other side of the lake was proving a great attraction.

We got seats in the sun on the upper deck and set sail for the second time for St. Gingolphe. I remember watching two buzzards with forked tails dive on to the surface of the lake for fish. Then I dropped off into a profound sleep to be woken by my family at St. Gingolphe. This time we had the sense not to disembark. We went down to the saloon to tea. Lalage refused to drink anything. I had my tea with lemon.

When I got back on deck I watched two wild duck, and then suddenly realised what a wonderful panorama of hills and gullies lies behind Montreux. Montreux itself seemed smaller than I had imagined. It is really all front. Its population is only eighteen thousand, an ideal size for a holiday resort.

We got off the steamer at Chillon. The whole inclusive fare for the four of us first-class came to less than ten francs.

We sat on the pierhead while Imogen tested the temperature of the water. She found it colder than she had expected. She was, as usual, dead honest in her opinion.

"I still think it's hot enough to bathe."

"It's cool enough to drink," I said. "I'm going across to the Taverne."

We sat in the sun in front of the Taverne watching the first loads of Sunday skiers returning from the hills. There was a good-looking young man in an Oxford blue sweater decorated with white at top and bottom. He drove up in an immense green open car and was accompanied by a bare-headed girl of great beauty in white jersey and light blue skiing trousers. She seemed to have a lot of make-up on, but she was most attractive. A very old woman in black accompanied by a tiny child hobbled across the road and took up her position at a table. A lonely gendarme occupied another.

Jill suddenly and irrelevantly burst into a rhapsody over Swiss public lavatories.

"Not only is there no trace of litter on any street, but the lavatories are spotless and they don't charge. In England they charge, presumably for the stink and the dirt."

Lalage urged her mother not to be vulgar.

I suddenly became desperately tired.

I listened listlessly to Lalage laying down the correct procedure in the writing of postcards.

"You mustn't begin," she said, "and you mustn't end."

"Leave out the middle," I said, "and save postage."

When later at dinner she reprimanded Imogen for picking up a goose bone and gnawing it she said,

"You'd never see anyone else in this hotel doing that."

"Yes, you would," retorted Imogen, "you'd see Daddy."

"No respectable people ever pick up bones in their fingers," said Lalage.

"You ought to write a series of books on etiquette," I said. "How to address postcards. How to behave at table. How to——"

I suddenly caught Jill's eye.

It was my tiredness. I realised that.

The dining-room was overpoweringly hot. I felt an overwhelming desire to go to bed. I hadn't enjoyed what I had eaten. I didn't even want another bottle of wine. I finished my iced banana and got up.

I said to Lalage:

"It's not done but I'm doing it. I'm going to bed."

In the hall I met the charming Mr. Alplas, the Director of Tourism.

"I'm going to take you out for a drink," he said.

I knew that he hadn't much leisure. I knew that he would help to fill out my picture. I tried to keep my eyes open.

"That's awfully good of you," I said.

"The family as well, of course."

"Of course."

"In ten minutes."

"In ten minutes."

I went upstairs and fell fast asleep.

I was woken by the family.

"There's a man in the hall says we're going for a drink," said Jill.

"That's quite right," I replied.

I hoped that we were going back to Hilda.

We didn't. We took a tram to the centre of Montreux and settled down in the twilight outside the Ravenaz watching more and more young things returning from the hills, skiers in white jerseys with skis over their shoulders, climbers in heavy boots and rucksacks on their backs. Lucky, lucky Swiss youth. No wonder they look so poised and have such perfect manners. They are in close communion with their lovely heights.

"What'll you have?" said our host to Lalage.

"Nothing, thank you," said Lalage.

"You can't have nothing. They don't have it."

I hadn't realised until that moment that I was in the presence of a wit.

For the next hour we were being richly entertained not only by drinks but by information and amusing stories.

Imogen settled down to a large glass of "sirop." So long as she was able to suck it through a straw she wouldn't have jibbed at brandy. "Sirop" is Swiss for Grenadine.

"I'm going round and round," she said joyfully.

A robust middle-aged man in a Tyrolean hat spun out of the interior uncertainly, smiled blandly at us and teetotumed round the corner.

"He's going round too," I said. "You're in good company."

Jill, our host, and I were drinking a potent liqueur made from the remains of the grape after it has been pressed for wine. It sounds like "marr" or "myrrh" and is spelt, I think, "maae." It tastes slightly bitter but it leaves one mellow.

"*A votre santé*," said our host.

"Cheers," said Jill.

"*Sköl*," said I.

After three "maaes" I felt better able to cope with the world.

"I've seen a swallow," I said.

"Why do your buzzards have kites' tails?" said Jill.

"I'm out of my depth," said our host. "I'm not a bird-man."

"What a pity," I said. "There's so much I want to find out about your birds."

Our host got up.

"Excuse me a minute."

I thought he had gone to the lavatory.

He returned smiling.

"I've fixed it for Wednesday. Herr Châtalenat will pick you up in his car at 9.45 and take you to the bird-watchers' hut at Villeneuve."

How typically Swiss that instant act of courtesy was.

Jill didn't say "You are an angel" solely because she was lost in contemplation of the cherry-brandy.

The talk turned, as talk will, on what you can take out of the country.

"You can take out five watches," he said.

"What about jerseys?" said Jill.

"So long as you wear them."

"What about shoes?" asked Lalage anxiously.

"So long as you wear them."

"I shall wear my playing-cards," said Imogen producing them and beginning to play patience.

"I want to buy an attaché-case," I said. "But I think two hundred francs too much."

"I'll tell you where to go," said our host.

"I think we'd better be going," said Jill.

"We haven't started yet," said our host.

We walked from the Ravenaz up the main street which to me, mellowed by three "maaes," seemed to be thronged with exceptionally fascinating females.

"In the hotel everyone," I said, "is over eighty. In the streets everyone is under eighteen."

We sat down in a garden outside the Bavaria.

"The idea of these bushes is to protect drinkers against the wind. It doesn't; only drink protects you against the wind. Let's go inside," said our host.

Inside I jostled a man to whom I was introduced. His name was Fischer. His brother, I was told, was a famous Davis Cup player.

We sat down in a medieval room with a very friendly atmosphere. The walls were decorated with enormous panels on which had been painted the Rhône falls, William Tell's house, blue lakes and snowclad peaks.

This time we drank Grand Marnier.

We were to have drunk Promiet, or Phum, but, well, you can't beat Grand Marnier, can you?

I had three. Imogen again spread out her playing-cards and gave an excellent entertainment.

At a late hour Lalage thawed and showed us her match trick. Our host, as I expected, was full of tricks. It was late when we got home. I don't remember going to bed.

Monday, 21st April, 1947

"THE rain always comes from Lausanne," said somebody. It arrived this morning at six o'clock. For two hours before that it had been fine.

One of the earliest birds this morning to get going was the buzzard, or was it a child crying?

Switzerland is an odd country.

I haven't seen more than half a dozen cats or three dozen dogs in ten days and I have met no Swiss man or woman who doesn't regard me as slightly eccentric for my love of birds. They don't know when the swallow comes or the name of the buzzard. There is a frail, elderly, but completely charming American woman in the hotel who said when I mentioned this, "What did you expect? They have something else to do."

So far as my very superficial knowledge goes the Swiss have natural good manners (I saw a workman in the bus this morning give two buttonholes of lilies of the valley to two young girls who I'm pretty sure were strangers to him), they are superb engineers and know how to get the last ounce out of their water ("Why is there no hot water, Daddy?" "Because there's no cold water"), they have an exquisite sense of taste in woodwork and dress, but far less (I guess) in literature and painting, they make and appreciate good wine and good food (but I should not describe them as *bons-vivants*), a few of them make millions, all of them make more than a competence, they are past-masters in the art of hotel-keeping, they know how to dress their shop-windows, and how to cultivate all their cultivable land, but they are not animal-lovers.

They like physical exercise and are, I imagine, tough as we are tough but not vulgar as we are vulgar, or (this is again a guess) immoral as we are immoral. Their monkey-parade is not a sexual parade. It is rather a parade of boys and girls of unusual physical attraction (to us) who are completely unconscious of that attraction.

The girls of Montreux—and Montreux is simply full of girls—paint their lips, wear extraordinarily short frocks and most alluring clothes, but they are most certainly not man-hunters. They appear to me to be completely chaste, even puritanical. Calvin's influence is still strong. They are all the more exciting on this account.

It would be very difficult to think of anyone making love to the shy fawn of a waitress who whispers her greetings to me in the hotel, or for that matter to the ebullient, ever smiling Hilda, who waits on me at the Chillon Taverne.

In the tram last night I said to Herr Alplas, who confessed to a great affection for London,

"You must find it very dirty and uncomfortable. We are rude and gauche, and very, very grim and tired."

"Tired? Yes," he said. "I find it very sad to think of England dying. You have done nothing to deserve it."

I was so completely taken aback that my first inclination was to throw him off the tram.

Dying? England dying? The thought had never so much as crossed my mind, as I imagine it has never crossed yours. The thought of a universe without England is unthinkable.

We are no more dying than we were in the days of the

Armada or Waterloo, but victory in war drains any nation's vitality.

We are still licking our wounds, and those wounds were severe. No Englishman believes that they were mortal. Every European believes that they were.

We spent the wet morning in the shops. I am rapidly coming to the end of my shopping, but even though I cannot afford to achieve a Swiss wrist-watch I am able to go home the richer by a brief-case.

I found a superb one this morning in light durable calfskin. It was a very handsome affair, all zippers, side-pockets and brass locks.

It had been slightly discoloured by the sun, and to my surprise the shopkeeper let me have it without tax for a hundred and fifty francs. I also succumbed to the lure of a complicated purse that opened out to display all one's loose cash on a stiff tray. That cost a sovereign.

Jill failed to find any underclothes, but to my indignation (I felt like Pepys) fell heavily for a gold ring at forty-eight francs. I told her that I hadn't enough money left for that. She countered by saying that I should have if I drank less. I replied that if I drank less I should pass out with tiredness. In the ring-shop I was entranced by an engagement-block on a slab which contained a large watch in the middle with space all round it for the day's appointments. An ideal present for a doctor.

We revisited the Catholic church and spent some time admiring six superbly carved and very colourful angels who rose out of a sea of almond-blossom, and six equally fascinating gold incense-censers. Nuns were worshipping in the side-chapels.

We went into the ornate Kursaal to visit the exhibition of modern paintings by Huessler and Berger. It was entirely deserted except for the custodian who couldn't speak or understand a word of English. I found Berger's work, mainly of nudes, crude, but Huessler extremely pleasant. Huessler's forte lies in portraits, especially of men. There was one of a strikingly handsome man with a fine bone-line which entirely captivated Jill. He also paints the Alps in rich colours and with vision. Only one of his pictures was marked VENDU. That was of a cup and saucer.

We spent some time in Herr Alplas's office arming ourselves with brochures of various Swiss resorts. The Swiss certainly know how to whet their prospective visitors' appetites. I was most attracted by a magnificently illustrated souvenir of the American G.I.'s Swiss leave. We ought to have produced a similar souvenir in Britain. It occurred to me that the American soldier must have been much less successful in his conquest of the Swiss miss than he was with the English.

We drank at the Bavaria, but it was deserted and, without the company of Alplas, lacked gaiety.

At luncheon I began my attack on the red wine. I selected for my first choice a bottle of Veltliner at 5 frs. 50 c. It was smooth, so smooth that I found myself mightily applauding Imogen who was playing with two tiny carved dogs on magnetic feet.

"I believe these dogs are allergic to each other," she said.

"Good God," I said.

"Haven't I used 'allergic' in its right sense?" she asked innocently.

"*Au contraire*," I said.

I went out on to the balcony. The clouds had passed over, leaving the air clean and sweet. The sun was blazing down. A young girl passed singing. She wore white stockings that ended below the knee, a white thick skiing sweater and a billowy check skirt. I felt at peace with the world and very happy. I fell asleep.

At two o'clock I was summoned back to life by the hoot of a motor-horn.

The motor-coach had arrived to take us to Villars.

"May we have," I asked, "the roof open?"

The driver opened it.

We had only driven two or three hundred yards before the driver was called upon to stop.

We were outside the Castle of Chillon.

A colourless Englishwoman left her seat and got out.

"It's too breezy altogether," she said pointedly, and so missed one of the most wonderful drives in all Europe.

It began simply enough down the flat green valley of the Rhône. I was getting used to the Rhône valley, but I had not before noticed the frequent fissures in the high rocks or the amount of blasting that goes on in the limestone quarries.

Imogen craned her neck to see if anybody was bathing at

Villeneuve from the Montreux Plage. She had of course, with her usual indomitable optimism, brought her bathing-costume and equally of course mine. She had read in the brochure of the magnificent open-air bathing-pool at Villars.

We passed (going the same way) several hundred jeeps and motor-bicycles containing extremely young Swiss soldiers. They waved genially as we drove past.

At Ollon I fell asleep, so I saw nothing of the view as the coach wound its way up the hillside to Villars, which stands four thousand feet up in the sun facing across the Rhône valley to the Dent du Midi.

It took Imogen quite a time to wake me from my slumbers.

I woke to realise that I was in a village street full of soldiers and empty jeeps. The soldiers were basking in the sun singing very melodiously and quite quietly songs of their native hills. I made my way into the post-office.

"I want," I said, "to find a chalet called Les Bruyères."

"It's in Chesières," said the girl, as if Chesières were a distant suburb.

"How far?" I asked.

"Just over the bridge," she said. "Five minutes."

When I first thought of coming out to Switzerland I had written to the proprietor of the Hôtel Belvedere at Chesières and his prices were so moderate that I very nearly fixed to go there, but from the brochure I gathered that Chesières was out of the swing of things in Villars. I couldn't have been more wrong. The village street is presumably the hub of Villars, and at the end of it stands a handsome school and beyond that a wide bridge spanning a deep ravine. On the further side I saw the Belvedere and a *pension* called Les Bruyères.

I gave a vigorous pull at a cunningly devised bell-pull. It looked exactly like a small broom for brushing the snow off one's feet. I pulled at it twice. It didn't give. It was a small broom devised for brushing the snow off one's feet.

"You are a fool, Daddy," said Lalage severely. She pointed to but did not ring the sort of electric bell that you see in Harley Street or Hartlepool. I took her advice. It rang.

"Why are we going in here?" asked Imogen. "Is this where you draw your pension?"

You know the way people give you addresses of people whom

you have never met. "You simply must meet John Corlette," said a friend of mine. "He's just your cup of tea."

After pressing the bell I wondered whether he was going to be my cup of tea.

Luckily Mr. Corlette was my cup of tea.

"Coming out for a cup of tea?" I said on greeting him.

"I'd love to," he said, and that was that. "Let me take you for a short walk to give you an appetite."

My heart sank as we set off in the opposite direction from that of the village, but it meant a closer view of the Belvedere, and we there turned up towards the wooded hills and found ourselves facing a very large and ultra-modern house with a flat roof that seemed to me all balconies and glass windows. Above the flat roof floated a flag.

"That's some nation," I said. "I ought to know it."

"Belgium," he said and kept all trace of superiority out of his voice.

"You were at Oxford," I said.

"Exeter."

"School?"

"Stowe." He pointed to the big house.

Vast crowds of extremely gay and healthy-looking children chased an escaping ball into a stream.

"Belgians?" I said.

"Refugees," he answered. "You should have seen them when they came."

"Skin and bone?"

"Not even that. Wraiths. Poor mites. I'm buying that house."

"Eve [our mutual friend] didn't tell me you were a millionaire."

"I teach two English boys."

"I didn't realise that teaching was so profitable."

"I'm proposing to make it so. I'm going to run this as an English public school."

He pointed to a hillside dotted with handsome chalets. He picked out three or four.

"When I get going I'm going to buy that and that and that and that."

"Out-Etoning Eton?" I said.

"There are a lot of boys in English public schools who don't fit."

"You are," I said, "informing me."

"I'd forgotten you'd been a public-school master. Sorry. I was at Gordonstoun for three years.

"When do you open?"

"I haven't bought it yet. The Bank of England is providing five thousand pounds."

"Uncommonly handsome of them. May I have their address?"

"It's the Swiss who are the snag. They dislike competition."

"Switzerland for the Swiss?"

"Exactly. You may spend money here. You mustn't earn it."

"That's a point of view."

"I spend my days appealing for permits and being refused."

"How like home," I said. "They won't let me repair my garden fence. Let it lay, they say, after Byron."

"The Swiss association of teachers say they have enough schools of their own."

"I have heard of Swiss schools."

"I say there's room for mine."

"I wish you luck."

"I've got to raise the money in Switzerland."

"A Herculean labour."

He snorted.

"If only it were as simple. The Swiss like money."

"Don't we all?"

"I want to start a school."

"You've said that."

We passed a mill full of flour-bags.

"I thought they imported all that," I said.

"They import butter, milk, meat, oil, coal, all sorts of things, but they are self-supporting in some products."

"Wood?"

"And flour here and there."

We passed a group of young girls. They were talking English.

We passed innumerable groups of small children.

Imogen waved her bathing-costume.

"Where are the baths?" she asked.

"We're coming to those," said Corlette.

We descended from the woods to face an enormous barracks called the Palace Hotel. It was shut.

We crossed an asphalt tennis-court to a huge swimming-pool with a fascinating chute and diving-boards to suit every taste.

Imogen stood still. There were tears in her eyes.

" Why, it's empty," she said.

Corlette had to agree.

" Isn't there enough water to fill it?" asked Imogen. " I don't believe the Swiss ever bathe."

I looked across the valley to the snow-clad Dent du Midi. The view was unbelievably good.

" I'd like to stay here," I said. " I like the openness and the view and the way the sun penetrates every cranny."

The soldiers sat by the grass verge singing.

The fields were yellow with cowslips and deep blue with gentians.

" Will you pick me a buttonhole?" I said to Imogen.

She handed me her bathing-costume and went off slowly towards the colourful fields.

" I feel more than ever the need of tea," I said.

We crossed the main street which seemed to be all railway-line and tram-line and Army and entered a restaurant. It was called Alpe des Fleuris.

The windows were shut and the rooms out of the sun.

" I must," I said, " be out of doors and in the sun. I hope I don't sound fussy. I've got to take sweetness and light back to England."

" I understand," said Corlette.

We opened and shut several doors and emerged on to a balcony, the only sunny corner of which was already occupied by the man from Lunn's and some fellow coach-travellers.

It was a matter of moments for me to crowd them all together and put my chair just where I wanted it.

My neighbour was an attractive girl who complained of the age of her fellow guests at the Excelsior.

" But," she said, " I can get my sun-bathing."

Imogen only caught the last word and nearly jumped the intervening tables.

" Where?" she said. " Oh, where?"

I left it to the attractive girl to prick that bubble.

Tea was long in coming. We had all too little time to explore the shops.

I fingered lovingly a gaberdine skiing suit. Jill bought a pair of white socks at seven-and-sixpence.

Corlette took Imogen off to buy for her a Lilliputian mouse carved in ivory.

I gazed at a number of brooches also carved in ivory, of mountain flowers, edelweiss and gentian.

I looked at my watch. It was 4.45.

"Time to go," I said to no one in particular.

I took a few photographs of distant mountains.

I boarded the bus.

"Don't," I said to Imogen, "let me go to sleep. I've not seen Villars yet."

"I won't," she said. "But you get so angry when——"

"I've never been known to be angry," I said.

The drive from Villars down to Bex is the most wonderful that I have encountered in Switzerland. The road is narrow. We kept on going within an ace of hurling oncoming jeeps over the precipice. Once or twice I thought that our driver would fail to make the turn at one or other of the hundred hairpin bends, but I was well content to die in the presence of such grandeur.

Villars looks nothing from below. It doesn't even look high, but the world, seen from Villars, is stupendous. I don't know the names of the peaks that we saw, but we looked down through the trees over two green ravines, with red-roofed chalets dotted about in the rich valleys to one great rocky mountain after another. There was just no end to the loveliness.

Occasionally we pulled up and I stood uncertainly on the seat and took photographs through the roof. Fifty or sixty miles away we could see the smooth snowy surface of Mont Blanc behind the Dent du Midi.

We came to Gryon with its scarlet-painted clock and medieval stone church tower. We crossed the railway and went round and round and round through Les Posses with its children's playground, washing-troughs and wood-piles. We ran through Fenelat where children, in blue smocks, sitting on a low wall under the white chalets, waved gaily as we passed.

We descended to the land of vineyards at Chêne, a hamlet

E

built on three bends of the road. We passed a salt mill and came to Bex, an unexpectedly large and prosperous-looking town with a river and great timber-yards, rich-looking hotels and corn on the cob hanging out to dry under the eaves of the chalets.

The streets of Bex are cobbled and there are trams. The shops looked inviting and the lilac was just flowering. One chalet was almost hidden under a profusion of clematis.

We looked up to the long straggling street of Villars. From the Rhône valley it gives no indication of its superb beauty.

We came once more to Aigle and the vineyards of Yvorne.

It took us just over an hour to get down from Villars to Chillon where Hilda was waiting for us with a happy smile and outstretched arms.

We sat on the balcony, drank Campari, and then climbed up the zigzag path behind to the open fortifications that had been carved in the rock-face.

Hilda told us of the six men who had been killed here during the war owing to an explosion. So Switzerland had had her war losses too.

I envied the guests who had the good fortune to have a table by the vast windows because God had painted His lake and hills and sky in quite unforgettable colours. The guests at the window tables, after one quick glimpse and saying how wonderful, were turning to their soup and champignons with fuller relish after their own fashion.

I let my food grow cold. I just had to watch the velvet hand of dusk quietly caress the dark hills. The lake silently and imperceptibly lost its blush and faded into a deep smooth oily mass of pearl and steel grey.

After dinner I walked with or rather in front of my slow-moving family towards the town. They gazed into so many shop-windows that I sat alone in Les Ravenaz for half an hour before they came. I ordered Yellow Chartreuse but the proprietor recommended La Grande Gruyère as being an excellent substitute.

Chartreuse cost two francs, La Grande Gruyère 1 fr. 50 c. Commenting loudly on this saving for Lalage's benefit I had three glasses.

"It's a waste of money whatever it costs," said Lalage, and went on writing letters.

Imogen produced her pack of cards and was soon lost in a game of patience.

By 9.30 I was in bed.

Tuesday, 22nd April, 1947

THE first bird sang at 4.30. At 4.45 two men below my window began to talk. At 5.30 they were still talking.

Under the cold clear light of dawn the Alps and the lake looked even lovelier than they had looked at sunset the night before. At sunset I have to share the scene with my fellow men. At dawn I share the glory with the birds who may be just as insistent on their territorial rights but are more melodious about it.

This was to be our high-spot day. Lunn's man had dinned into me, and Rudolph the hall porter had corroborated Lunn, that the Red Arrow excursion simply had to be taken.

This was to be the first Red Arrow excursion of the year. It runs on Tuesdays only. It is a neat idea and typical of the Swiss.

At 8.10 you board a luxury train with observation cars and are whirled along at eighty miles an hour down the Rhône valley as far as Brig, whisked up the mountain-side through the Lötes-berg tunnel which is ten miles long to emerge in German Switzer-land at Kandersteg. You are then given a chance to get some exercise by walking to see the famous Blue Lake, rejoin the train to run down to Interlaken for luncheon, race alongside Lake Thun to take a coach ride round Berne for tea and so home by way of Friburg at 6.40. The cost, third-class, is twenty-five francs with three francs extra for the coach trip.

It sounds magnificent. It must have sounded magnificent to about five hundred other people, for on arrival on Montreux platform at eight o'clock I found it as full as Croydon platform at 8.40 or Oxford at 10.15 daily. I didn't like the look of that crowd, though a large contingent of them were Swiss schoolboys.

Imogen went almost mad with delight at finding a fellow Dragon. We joined parties, making eight of us in all. The Cook's man took his party to the rear of the train. The Lunn's man led us to the front. We occupied the whole of the leading coach and congratulated ourselves on our superb judgment because we had an uninterrupted view of the line and country in front. Our triumph was short-lived for a reason that you can guess.

For a hardened traveller I am unduly fussy. I fussed over getting my family through their breakfast in time to catch the train to the station. I was apprehensive lest the train should fail to come. Both these worries were needless. We caught the train easily and we got the best seats. We set off at a terrifying rate and as far as Bex I have nothing new to report. We were by now accustomed to the opening of the Rhône valley.

In spite however of the fact that I had made it clear that I had to work I was given little opportunity to take notes. Everybody had so much to say about irrelevant things that I only managed to keep an intermittent look-out.

Lunn's man came round selling maps of the route but hadn't any left by the time he came to me. I almost raised the roof off the train, so he found one somewhere, and by the time we reached Martigny I knew where we were. It was here that the Rhône makes a mighty sweep left-handed and we with it.

There were colossal peaks rising on either side as we ran through the wide flat valley of orchards to Saxon where I noticed that all the trees were being blown sideways by the winds from the north-west.

We passed an aerodrome at Sion, but I was more interested in a medieval monastery standing inaccessibly on the top of a rocky knoll cheek by jowl with the walls of an old castle that stood on an adjoining rock. The slopes of the hill leading to the monastery were covered with vineyards. The Rhône, now clear and light, green and broad, ran alongside the railway-line which was now single. At Sierre we ran into a land of scrub and stunted trees, rather like the Painted Desert.

At Leuk I got very excited at the sight of a small black animal that was racing along a narrow track on the hillside. I gave it all sorts of names until one of our party announced that it was a dog. I felt that my stock had fallen.

The river here had a white sandy beach. "Just the place," said Imogen, "to bathe." There was nobody bathing. I noticed that the carts were all drawn by mules. A white church with a red spire on a hill marked the approach to Visp.

I craned my neck out southwards for a view of Zermatt, Saas Fée, Monte Rosa and the Matterhorn, but the valley that led to them was narrow and the view beyond shut out by nearer hills.

At Brig we came to the entrance of the Simplon tunnel which was also invisible, and here I saw the reason for Cook's man taking his contingent to the back of the train. We now became the rear of the train and remained so for the rest of the day. This was a pity as the high spot of the journey was about to begin. We backed out of Brig in the direction from which we had come but along a line which climbed steeply along the hill-side on the north of the valley. The view quickly grew wilder. We entered and left behind about twenty tunnels before turning away north above Gampel to penetrate the heart of the Alps. We now ran above precipitous ravines in a land of silver birches and impressive waterfalls. Time and again we had false alarms that we had entered the long tunnel of Lotschberg.

We saw a mountain road that in one place had become completely blocked by an avalanche, and at Goppenstein we waited for a long time outside the Lotschberg tunnel waiting for a train to come through from the other side. All the notices were in German.

Two fraus were at work manuring their rhubarb-bed just outside the station. We all felt thirsty but dare not leave the train to find the buffet knowing as we did the Swiss rule about sending a train out at the advertised time regardless of any passengers still standing on the platform.

At last the other train came in. Lalage started her stopwatch and we entered the famous tunnel. When we re-emerged into the light of day at Kandersteg Lalage announced that the time was ten minutes two seconds.

I looked out on high precipitous rocks. There was very little green slope. I wondered why Kandersteg had achieved such a name among skiers.

We ran down swiftly towards the Blue Lake, and Lunn's man came along to tell us first that it was on the right, then on the left, and finally that it was on the right. It was on the left.

When eventually we were told to get out Imogen took her bathing-things.

" Probably," she said, " there's a bathing-place open here."

She ran on ahead. I loitered behind to scan the snow-line and forest edge for chamois. It looked to me ideal chamois country. We were told by the Cook's man that we had fifty minutes but not how far we had to go. I wanted a drink as well as chamois. It was a steep walk down a valley that was richly green. Everywhere farm-workers were sprinkling the land with dry and liquid manure. They even used a motor-car for the purpose. The fields were not only a rich green, they were carpeted with cowslips.

I let the party get so far ahead that I lost my way, but a passing motorist came to my rescue. Groups of small children (you will hardly believe this) stood by the roadside trying to sell us bunches of heather. It was like Piccadilly Circus.

I came to a well-worn track among mossy boulders in a pine wood and soon I was looking down on a small silent pool that did indeed reflect the blue of the sky. It had a white bottom and was full of trout. Nearby was a trout farm with more pools crammed with thousands upon thousands of extremely handsome blue trout. The blue of the water had impregnated their scales. I looked for a drink. The Gasthaus was shut. The season hadn't started. I began to climb towards the station and found a beer-house open. I drank some ice-cold lager only to be reminded by Cook's man that I had only five minutes more. I refused to leave my beer and only caught the train by running over the manured fields. "Isn't there a lovely smell of grass?" said Imogen.

I then settled down to my prodigious packed luncheon as I looked out over a well populated and fertile valley of red-roofed chalets. We raced through Frutigen where the large platform seemed to be full of business-men carrying brief-cases, and I looked out for the first signs of the Mönch, Eiger and Jungfrau. A broad clear river of green ran merrily alongside the railway-line as far as Spiez where we turned right-handed and ran along the shore of Lake Thun which was dotted with a series of very handsome villas. I saw one grey wagtail and a few swallows. Most of the chalets were surrounded by cherry-trees in full bloom, and there were fishermen on the lake in rowing-boats.

And so we came to Interlaken below the high Alps, and dispersed in search of shops and drinks. I bought postcards and something from a chemist whose shelves were lined with stuffed ravens, kingfishers, weasels, owls, buzzards and other hawks.

We wandered in search of a place to sit out in the sun and

found all the big hotels facing the green and the sun closed. Imogen went off with her school-friend. Lalage wandered off to the shops alone. I retraced my steps to Krebbs Hotel where I drank Campari at twice the price I pay in Montreux. I could just see the top of the Jungfrau and nothing else. I was disappointed with Interlaken. It was too German, and there was nothing to see. "Vastly overrated," said Jill. "Give me Montreux." "Me too," said I.

I was glad to re-enter the train and to retrace our track along the lakeside (the same side) by way of Spiez to Thun, where I looked up to see a most romantic-looking white castle with turrets and red roofs standing above a lot of factories. I was told that they made ammunition here.

I was more interested in a smart white steamer that was moored up alongside the station.

We left the Alps behind and I went to sleep. I was woken, not easily, at Berne, where Lalage had been left behind so long ago on our outward journey. We boarded one of two motor-coaches and were driven through very modern, very wide streets with dull uniform putty-coloured fronts to see the Federal Palace, Casino, Treasury, a gymnasium, the British Embassy which flew no flag, and the Brazilian Embassy which flew a green and black one. We passed several neat suburban villas. There was no one about. This part of the town was quite deserted. We passed a rose garden and looked across the River Aar which was broad and deep and a clear green, to see the massive towers and spire of the cathedral. Berne, like Shrewsbury, is almost encircled by a horseshoe-shaped river. We stopped by one of the bridges and Lunn's man said that we had ten minutes. He didn't say what for. I followed the crowd who were standing in a semicircle peering down into a pit. It was a bear pit. There were three brown bears, all putting on an act.

One was perched high up on a pole pretending that he was afraid of falling. One was walking round and round stopping every time he came to the closed iron door of his cage to stand on two legs and throw his head back to express indignation and sorrow at his repeated frustration. One just sat up and begged, and cleverly caught carrots in one paw. These carrots were being thrown to him by the generous visitors who bought them from an apple-faced old woman close by.

"I told you there were bears in Switzerland," I said to Imogen. "You owe me five shillings."

There were models of bears everywhere. Berne seemed to be bear-mad.

We rejoined the coach and I looked out over the bridge to see steep green slopes down to the river. We came to the old part of the town, which was a tremendous and complete change.

In the first place it was thronged. In the second it was colourful. The middle of the street was taken up by a succession of images of very gay knights in armour carrying flamboyant pennons of gold and silver. On either side were rich-looking shops under stone arcades or cloisters, like the Rows in Chester, reached by steps.

We came to a building with a vast gilt clock and under it I saw a clock showing the phases of the moon. We drove round the cathedral square and pulled up to admire the rich stone carving of the Last Judgment on the western front. To my great indignation and Jill's amusement we were not offered a chance to inspect the interior of the cathedral.

"Ten minutes for the bears but no time for God," said Jill.

We were put down by the Federal Palace and told abruptly to find our way back to the station. Luckily we were opposite a colourful open-air market with booths roofed with awnings of red and white stripes. I saw a tea-shop with red umbrellas shading the tables on the terrace. I entered it and found it occupied by about half England. There was a tremendous scrum at the pâtisserie counter and a bewildering choice. I planted my family down in ones and twos at any vacant table I could find and, infuriated by their inability to announce a choice, piled a plate high with dainty-looking pâtisserie and returned to the tables to find that I had got none of the delicacies they wanted. I only wanted a drink. For that I had to wait on the caprice of the waitress who as usual misunderstood my order. A Salvation Army lassie came round selling papers. I asked her to get me a glass of tea. She looked surprised. When the waitress arrived she had forgotten the lemon and my hot water. I saw some lovely frothy stuff in a glass which I mistook for iced coffee and ordered it. The waitress brought two immense coffee ices. Lalage doesn't like coffee. Imogen was nearly sick trying to swallow hers.

"I wish you wouldn't waste so much money, Daddy," Lalage said.

A Swiss boy and girl sharing my table had long finished, but out of politeness refused to rise till I did. They told me that the name of the restaurant was Bäreck and that if I wanted to buy things cheaply I ought to visit Loeb.

In the end I got up and went off alone to take photographs of the great gilt clocks. I saw a shop filled with every variety of sausage-meat, typically German, I saw watch-shops, knife-shops, leather goods, jewellery. I was glad that Jill was not with me. I fought my way back through a vastly overcrowded street to the station which was thronged with passengers. I couldn't find the Red Arrow. I had forgotten that it was red. There was only two minutes to go and I panicked. Porters looked at me with blank faces as I shouted, "The 5.5 for Montreux. Where is it?" I was led to the stationmaster's office and made myself unpopular by interrupting a clerk who was telephoning. No one had ever heard of Montreux, and there was no 5.5. I began running, in spite of DANGER DE MORT notices, across the railway-line. Then in the distance I spotted a red train, and dodging in and out between trains that seemed to be moving in every direction I achieved my car only to see the Lunn's man standing imperturbably smiling.

"Had a good day?" he asked.

The train started and I sat alone looking out on the distant Alps.

They increase in grandeur as they get further away. The intervening land is rolling pleasant country, not unlike Sussex, but with this difference.

After racing along at eighty-five miles an hour we pulled up at a tiny hamlet called Rosé.

On the other side of the platform was a Restaurant du Gare.

The windows were open and there was a crowd inside, obviously enjoying a very good dinner.

You try to get a dinner or a meal of any sort in a Sussex village. We don't know the first thing about the art of entertaining visitors.

We passed Jersey cattle at grass wearing cow-bells. We ran through Friburg, where a wide bridge over the river divides German from French Switzerland, and I was glad to leave the

German cantons behind. I felt a strong desire to get out and explore the vast church and castle behind the town walls.

We passed medieval castles and monasteries and vast châteaux all perched high upon isolated rocks, and at last drew nearer to our own Alps and looked down on the still blue waters of Lake Léman and the sweet houses of Montreux. I felt as if I were coming home.

I had seen a large part of Switzerland in the last ten hours but nothing at all comparable in grandeur or softness to Montreux.

I was glad to sink into a chair outside the Metropole and drink Campari as I looked at the fishermen on the lake.

After dinner I walked down in the dark more than half asleep to drink more Campari at the Taverne du Château de Chillon.

Hilda had gone to bed. Otherwise life was perfect. Lights twinkled across from the feet of the Savoy Alps. Lights blazed along the hillside above Montreux. The Alps blackened, and I walked home in the sweet air well content and nine-tenths asleep.

Wednesday, 23rd April, 1947

IT rained heavily during the night and a sudden gale got up and blew the curtains and the windows to and fro.

By seven o'clock the lower slopes of the Savoy showed up bright green as the sun came over the hills. The upper slopes were wreathed in white cloud but the snow-clad peaks shone in the sun.

We were to have gone to Villeneuve to see the birds, but our guide Herr Châtalenat came in at eight o'clock to say that it was too wet in the marshes.

He told me that the bird I had mistaken for the buzzard was the black kite. He told me that the swallow was fast disappearing from Montreux because the modern roads made it too difficult to secure material for building his nests. He told me that he had seen a few swifts and that the other varieties of wagtail were all common on the lakeside. He advised me to go up to Glion and walk down the Gorge of Les Chardrants.

I rang up the headmistress of St. George's, Clarens, Miss

Southwell, who was up at Oxford in my time, and fixed to see her at 10.30.

Mr Brown of Lunn's gave me good advice about the return journey, to buy a flask of milk and coffee at Basle and also to take rolls and butter across France.

A man from Montana was very angry because snow had been falling all night above three thousand feet and he wants to go up again, and now can't.

Today is St. George's Day and Shakespeare's birthday, and it has been one of the most memorable days of my life, but we put out no flags even in Montreux where you hear more English spoken than French.

It appears also to be the beginning of the Summer Term. I watched countless children pass from the hour of 7.30 wearing very neat satchels on their backs, one covered with tiger hide. He would have been lynched for that idiosyncrasy in an English school. All the Swiss carry their goods on their backs. All the workers in the fields walk about with pannier baskets on their backs, and I have seen girls bicycling with milk churns strapped to their backs.

I have been wondering about the sex life of the Swiss. Though they speak French in Montreux they have few if any French habits. They don't spit, they don't leer. The men certainly don't ogle the women, nor do the women ogle the men. The girls, as I have repeatedly said, are uncommonly attractive physically, and they begin to use lipstick at an abnormally early age. They dress smartly and have a natural good taste, but they seem to dress to please themselves, not to attract admiration from the other sex. I have seen no necking after dark, and the American G.I. who practised an exhibitionist trick by riding up and down the main street on a bicycle this morning, singing loudly, elicited encouragement only from the English. He obviously was an object of disgust to the Swiss.

After breakfast we took a train to Clarens which lies on the lake shore on the other side of Montreux. L'Ecole St. Georges stands on a knoll surrounded by green fields of long rough grass. It is a modern flat-roofed building that is nearly all windows.

Miss Southwell, the headmistress, greeted me with a genial smile and showed us over. I was struck, as I expected to be, by the cleanliness and the light.

The school, which has fifty English girls and fifty girls drawn from other nations, is divided into two houses called Minerva and Diana. The girls feed together in an attractive square dining-hall, and are taught in classrooms each with twelve desks.

Many of the rooms are decorated with very colourful friezes, one depicting the girls in a blue uniform playing their summer games, another depicting winter sports. The notice-board was full of Swiss greetings telegrams, much more tasteful and colourful than ours.

Some of the girls sleep in dormitories for two, others in dormitories of six. The chapel has a terra-cotta pottery altar from Oberammergau, and the sick bay opens out on to a sun-terrace from which the invalids can watch the games going on below.

Miss Southwell told me that among the birds found near the school are the hoopoe and golden oriole.

Her charges are about three hundred pounds a year.

As we left the school Lalage burst out into a diatribe. " I think I must be allergic to schools," she said.

We had luncheon punctually at 12.30 and drank Dole, Clos du Mont, an extremely smooth red wine. The main dish was a delicious medley of egg, bacon, asparagus and potato which we had to bolt in order to catch our train at Territet.

By bullying I got the family away by one o'clock and much too full of good food we started to walk very quickly the mile to the station. Lalage started off in front to buy the tickets but dropped the money. I started to run after her, and Jill, who knows the capricious behaviour of my heart, shouted at me to stop. Imogen, who was with her, made some comment which caused Jill to turn on her and Imogen burst into tears, her first tears in Switzerland. I ran back to her.

" I won't have tears," I protested, " in Switzerland."

" I'm not crying, Daddy," she said, her face wet, but not with sweat.

I ran after Lalage and caught her up in the ticket-office where her way was blocked by some cow-faced English school-girls who were in the middle of an argument with the ticket-man. I simply shoved them aside. Lalage would have waited for ever.

"I've got a train to catch," I said, a fairly obvious comment. The English girls were surprised into dumbness. I got my ticket and caught the train, which was due to arrive at 1.12 and did, by the skin of my teeth.

My heart started its tricks. Jill was furious, a fury which was intensified as the train pulled up at Chillon station.

" What a fool you are," she said. " We could have caught it here without having to run at all."

" The manager said ' Territet,' " I replied. " Most of the trains don't stop here."

" This one does; you should have looked it up."

" It would have been cheaper too," said Lalage. " You do waste money, Daddy."

I felt sick. Lalage had hiccups. Imogen was on the verge of crying again. Jill looked furious.

It was a propitious start.

The bells on the station engine announced the departure of the train.

" Just like the angels," I said. Dead silence.

" Look where the new snow's fallen," I said. Dead silence.

" I wonder how everybody in the hotel knew that a foot of snow had fallen in the night above three thousand feet?" Dead silence.

We swung into the Rhône valley, and my heart sang at the signs of the sweet spring after the rain.

There were foals at Roche.

" Foals," I said to Imogen.

She never fails to be thrilled by the sight of a horse.

She smiled. I felt that the family was thawing out.

My heart was beastly and the whole world was going round very unpleasantly.

There was lilac in full flower at Yvorne.

" Look at the lilac," I said.

The colour in Jill's cheeks became less pronounced.

There was sun and snow and green pastures. It was all incredibly lovely.

The ticket-man came through and took away our tickets, calling out softly the name of the next station.

At Aigle two tough-looking anglers with immense rucksacks on their backs and wearing shining black gaiters went off to fish.

" Nous apportons tout pour chez vous," I read aloud from an advertisement of a man in blue uniform.

There was a florist's shop on the platform filled with flowers in pots. " Coals to Newcastle," I said.

Bright yellow trolleys were being trundled up and down full of milk churns.

At St. Tryphon I watched a merry party emerge from the Café Restaurant de la Gare.

I looked up at Villars which looked nearer than ever. We arrived at Bex. The time was 1.45. There was no sign of Corlette. I thought that I had given myself heart trouble for nothing. I ran round and round the station. Then I saw the family entering a car which was closed and looked much too small. It is unwise to judge by appearances. The car was a Lancia, and Corlette, into whose hands I was entrusting the lives of my beloved family, was the best driver and the fastest I have ever met. We set off down the Rhône valley, and my first feeling was that I was seeing Switzerland for the first time.

The train is no good, the motor-coach is no good, the small private motor-car is very good.

We came to St. Maurice where we crossed the Rhône at the Swiss Redoubt; there is a tall fortress with gay white and red shutters built on a rock commanding the defile.

There is also a grotto, le Grotte des Fées—the Grotto of the Fairies.

" It may be open," said Corlette. " It's full of stalactites and stalagmites."

" I was brought up on caves," I said, " in Derbyshire. I'm for the sun. I'll sit on the bridge . . ."

My family disappeared into the mountain-side and I was not sorry to let them go. We weren't getting on at all well, and I was feeling as if I might drop dead at any second. I walked half-way across the bridge and looked down a hundred and fifty feet into the murky green depths. An easy job, and not altogether unpleasant, to dive in. I had had a good life. I'd like it to end among the high hills where I felt so serenely happy. I was brought back to life by a wasp. I am afraid of wasps. This wasp developed a passion for me. It followed me across the bridge three times. I crossed to the Gendarmerie de Vaud where an Alsatian lay chained in the doorway.

I heard someone across the valley cry " cuckoo." It was not a bird. It was one child hiding from another. I was attracted by a tall roadside crucifix. I climbed down to the waterside by a steep track that was alive with lizards.

I looked miles up and heard noises that were familiar and very dear to me, the calls of my children. I could only just descry them with the aid of my glasses. They appeared to be on a terrace in front of a long, yellow two-storeyed bungalow with red shutters.

I read the name RESTAURANT GROTTE DES FÉES.

We all waved and shouted and the passing lorries and cyclists stopped to see the fun. The family disappeared and I fell asleep. Long after I woke up and recrossed the bridge, emptying my pockets of orange peel and glittering three-ply cigar-cases.

There was no sign of the family.

I saw a man running towards me and I thought it was Corlette coming to tell me that Imogen had fallen down into a bottomless lake in the grotto. I know these grottos. Then I saw the car.

" I think I'm allergic to grottos," said Lalage who looked pale. Imogen was very silent. They are both inclined to be car-sick and I was having constant reminders of running in the hot sun on top of a too heavy lunch.

We drove at lightning speed through St. Maurice, past a nunnery and some factories and so to Eviannez where the streets are cobbled and medievally narrow. I looked up the mountain-side to see and hear an enormous white cataract dropping thousands of feet.

" Pissevache," said Corlette. " Well named."

I guessed at the name and agreed.

So through Mieville where I caught a glimpse of the narrow black entrance to the Gorge du Trient, a fearsome place like a scene in the Inferno. We crossed a very lovely covered-in wooden bridge to Martigny. Martigny is one of the most romantic junctions in the world, for it is here that the Rhône turns abruptly left to the wide green valley that leads to Brig and the Simplon tunnel. Up the valley to the right lies the great St. Bernard Pass, and we took the road to Chamonix to climb to the Clos de la Forclaz. Corlette had kept quiet about it, but I realised that we were embarking on an extremely dangerous journey. I lost count of the number of hairpin bends after thirty and decided to have a bet on the way down that they exceeded fifty. You have to remember that this track is muddy, that it is hedgeless, and that if you make a mistake you fall over several thousand feet of precipice. Luckily I have no nervous fears of this sort of thing.

I adored every minute of the climb. The children were silent. They were, I think, feeling too sick to be frightened. We climbed up through the hamlet of La Fontaine, crazy hamlets perched precipitously among very green fields that had been well drained, up through Le Cergneaux, where I noticed a mill hut and a saw-mill. There were crucifixes everywhere. I saw one right on the far mountain top.

We got out of the car and sat in a field of wild crocuses and looked miles down over the wide green valley of the Rhône towards the far Alpine peaks whose tops were all sprinkled with glittering icing. It stopped about halfway down and the bases were all black. In the field below us a swarthy peasant in a straw hat worked unremittingly with a pick heaving away at the good earth. His wife, a bronzed hatless Amazon, passed with a pannier basket slung on her back. Their daughter, a dark-haired buxom girl wearing (of all things) spectacles, sat in midfield and did nothing.

" Will no one tell me what she thinks?" I said.

" She's thinking of nothing," said Corlette. " She just sits and grows like the gentian. She has all time on her hands."

We were there for a quarter of an hour and the girl never moved. I began to think that she was an image of the Blessed Virgin.

Larks were singing in the blue above. There were sweet-smelling cowslips, pansies, violets, crocuses and gentians everywhere.

We could hear the roar of unseen waters.

Far below lay the clustered white roofs of Martigny.

" I thought Martigny was a drink," said Lalage.

" It is," I said, " a most exhilarating drink."

I looked through the glasses at the mountain-tops, glittering in the sun. The snow on one ridge was transparent.

We re-entered the car and continued to negotiate hair-raising hairpin bends.

Eventually we reached the summit of the pass at the Clos la Forclaz. There was of course an hotel with green shutters. It was called the Hôtel du Clos de la Forclaz.

There was a crucifix bearing a plate which ran:

"A la douce mémoire de R^d Ch^{re} JOSEPH DELEZE, Curé de Trient, mort du pied de cette croix le 11 février 1944."

"What a lovely place to die," I said.

"What did he die of, Daddy?" said Imogen.

"Heart disease, climbing after a too heavy lunch."

"I feel sick," said Imogen and sat down suddenly in a field of wild crocuses.

"I feel cold," said Lalage and started a bout of hiccups.

I lifted up my eyes to the wild smooth snow-clad heights on the other side of the gully.

"Untouched and untouchable," said Jill. "How glorious."

It was indeed glorious. Eastward we looked five thousand feet down to the broad valley of the Rhône towards Brig, westwards we looked towards Chamonix and Mont Blanc. We could almost throw a stone into France.

A mule went sauntering past. I scanned the heights for chamois. I watched men sawing wood and walked down to another hotel below the summit. It was closed. Corlette ordered tea from the woman at the Hôtel de la Forclaz. Propped up against its sunny wall sat a pretty red-faced peasant girl smiling. She never took her gaze from us, but she never opened her mouth. She just went on smiling in the sun. I took a number of photographs and came to the end of my roll of films. I was carrying a spare roll and began to unpack it in the shade of the hotel. When I had removed all the paper I realised that it was not contained in a carton. I had let the light in and ruined the lot.

"You are wasteful, Daddy," said Lalage.

I was more than wasteful. I was plain idiotic, for a few minutes later I caught sight of a toy village far down at the foot of the defile leading to Chamonix. It had a tall white church, and the chalets of the flock over whom Joseph Deleze ruled. It was cut off from the world and from the sun. It was an indescribably lovely ravine and formed the other end of the fearsome Gorge du Trient that I had seen years before at Eviannez on the way through.

It would have made a superb photograph.

"We shall never come here again," said Jill.

"You're always getting hunches," said Lalage.

"I am very sure that I shall," I said, "as a ghost. It is the loveliest place that God has ever allowed me to see."

"What about the Grand Canyon?" said Jill.

"There are no tourists or cowboys or Indians to spoil it here," I said.

A tourist appeared at that moment, his arrival synchronising with that of tea and apricot jam.

"*Bon appétit,*" he said.

"Let good digestion wait on appetite," I added. My prayer was answered, for Imogen and Lalage both recovered as quickly as one snaps one's fingers. They demanded Toblerone which they hadn't seen since Woolacombe days in 1939.

They got a slab of something that contained honey and tasted just as good.

They both ate a prodigious tea and then Lalage went on writing her diary.

Imogen raced over the crocus fields to hide. There is something in the sight of her running over Alpine fields that makes me want to cry.

"There's something about a hill," said Corlette.

We were in our shirt-sleeves. Lalage now acknowledged that it was hot.

We stayed till the sun dipped over the western peaks. Within ten seconds the temperature had sunk to freezing-point.

There is certainly something about hills.

It was at that point that Corlette told us that the climb to the Clos de la Forclaz is considered to be the most dangerous, as it is certainly the steepest, in Europe.

"One in five," he said.

I listened to a woodpecker. Imogen played with two black cats. I gave up coupons for my tea. I gazed up at the mammoth massifs and felt like kneeling down. I thanked God on my feet in silence instead. Imogen went over to the washing-trough and began playing with a child's toy boat. I brought out my camera. It was no good.

"It's wonderful," she said, "for torpedoing," and wet herself thoroughly experimenting.

She then borrowed my new very sharp knife and began carving her name on a bench.

"We've got to go," I said. "I'll bet you sixpence there are more than fifty hairpin bends."

We started on the perilous downward journey exactly at six

o'clock. I lost my bet. There were forty-one hairpin bends. We argued fiercely about the difference between a traverse and a hairpin. The views were quite indescribable. We passed boulders and traces of avalanches, storm-bent trees and an endless number of labourers at work in the fields. We came back to civilisation, or at any rate the world of men, at Martigny which seemed as large as London.

Corlette accelerated to eighty. We flew past the Pissevache, we passed through orchards, avenues of tall poplars and hit a sudden howling gale sweeping down the Rhône valley like a train rushing through a Tube. The cobbled streets of Eviannez were full of small children. We didn't slow down.

There were children everywhere standing in doorways holding out outstretched hands full of lilies of the valley.

We passed under a gigantic rock.

"Valhalla," said Corlette.

We passed several nuns and saw a track marked LAVEZ.

"Salt baths," said Corlette.

After St. Maurice the land changed suddenly. It became softer. At Bex we came to more salt baths and salt mines, and beyond Ollon saw the police hold up all approaching cars.

They let us through.

"Why?" asked Lalage.

"We're British," said Corlette.

It seemed a satisfying answer.

The chestnuts were all in blossom at Aigle.

"The wine's good here," said Corlette. "They take it young. If they let it mature it would beat all the wine in France."

We came to a land of many Jersey cattle each tinkling its cow-bell musically.

We arrived at our lake. I felt as if I had come home.

"You see that tree islanded in the middle?" said Corlette. "That's a British possession. It was given by the Swiss to Queen Victoria."

We pulled up at the Taverne du Château de Chillon exactly as the clock struck seven.

"An hour," said Corlette. "Not bad going. She holds the road."

Hilda came out to greet us as if we had been away for a month. Corlette looked puzzled at her effusiveness. He recommended Amer Picon. We stuck to Campari. Lalage decided to walk home. Imogen stayed to drink soda-water. She seemed doubtful of its efficacy.

At the hotel I was met by Lunn's man who presented me with the account for the Red Arrow trip and the drive to Villars. In all they came to 126 frs. 50 c. for the four of us.

We went in to dinner and ate an extraordinarily well cooked perch. Crowds gathered at the window to watch God's nightly miracle of the sunset.

Above the black ridge of the western hills there were ridges of pure gold, above them a sea of bluey-green. The roof of the sky was rose-tinted, fading to pearl grey. All this was reflected in the water. The show lasted from 7.30 to 8.

"This is excellent perch," said Corlette. "You should try féver."

Jill started a discussion about constitutional government. Lalage decided that she must work. Jill and Imogen went to the pictures. Corlette took Lalage off to help her with her English précis. I moved about restlessly in the library and found a copy of my first novel *Interlude*.

I didn't like what I read inside. I picked up *Country Life* and found a very handsome review of my latest book. I picked up a brochure of Montreux. This is what I read: "To its guests. Ah, how lovely to do nothing! There are periwinkles and lilies of the valley in the woods, it rains brown, polished chestnuts under the chestnut-trees of Sonchaud. In the meadows of Les Avants, Caux, Chamby, the starry narcissus is more plentiful than the stars of heaven. Even the lake has the colours of flowers, of gentians and of syringa. In the gardens the magnolias with their white and rose egglike blossoms come to full flower. White sails fleck the rediscovered lake, while the gulls accost the first steamers which bring them scraps from the breakfast table. There is something in the air, something we cannot define, an enchantment which goes in quest of the sun. It is the soul of the holiday spirit which awakens with the Montreux sky. On the lake shore from Clarens to Montreux, on the path along the lake from Territet to Chillon, the first flowers of the acacias and the first summer frocks greet each other. The reflection of the lake through the many open windows dances on innumerable hotel bedroom ceilings. Montreux, between its huge tapestry of woods and its vast carpet of water, unfolds its deck-chairs, prepares its tennis-courts, brings out the chairs in front of the tea-shops, engages its orchestras, puts the cloths on the tables, polishes up its little excursion trains, yellow and blue for the Rochers de Naye, pearl grey for Blonay, purple for Glion, grey and white for Les Avants, the Pays d'En-Haut, the Gruyère, a colour for each horizon. The season of a thousand and one temptations is open and Montreux is always the rendezvous of good weather and a good time."

How succinct, how apt, how colourful, I thought. I specially liked the reminder of the different colours of the trains.

I stopped Corlette before he fell asleep. I took Lalage up to bed.

" I think he's wonderful," she said.

I led her to the window of my bedroom.

A new moon hung in the starry black sky.

"There's no husbandry in heaven tonight," I said.

We bowed solemnly nine times and turned our silver over as we silently wished.

"Does it matter if it's Swiss money?" asked Lalage.

" God accepts all currency," I said.

My heart was full of thankfulness.

I wonder if you can guess my wish.

Lalage settled down in bed to write up her diary.

Thursday, 24th April, 1947

IT is many years since I have slept as I slept in Montreux. Immediately my head touched the pillow whether I went to bed at nine or twelve I fell asleep. My dreams, if I had any, for the first time for at least twenty years, were completely free of frustration. I dream practically every night in England and always it is with a sense of some horrible obstacle put in the way of whatever it is I dream of doing. My dreams in Switzerland for that fortnight were all sweet dreams. I have no idea what they were about, but I do know that I liked having them. They were like the people, clean and serene. The fact that I woke at two, three or four in the morning is irrelevant. When I woke I immediately started to work, and as it was the only opportunity to work that I got I welcomed it. Dawn is the best time of day for me. I cannot work at night. My brain never functions in the evening. The birds were later with their dawn chorus during those last few days. That may have been due to the rain. It was sunny during the day for the whole of my visit, but it had rained at night for the last three nights. When Jill woke she complained of feeling sick. She lay in bed very sorry for herself all the morning. When I went to wake Imogen I found that she had been sick at 1.45, but I roused her and took her with Lalage on a shopping expedition, though she looked a bit green until I got her a dose at a chemist's.

This was mainly a financial morning.

I was reduced to 200 francs, and Boenski, the proprietor, told me that I owed him 160 francs for drinks and tea in the hotel. I had still my luggage to register and two days to go and the bank told me last week that I could cash no more traveller's cheques. As however I wanted to get my photographs developed I bearded the bank in the hope of getting round that somehow, and discovered to my delight that they were willing to let me have five pounds' worth more of vouchers, that is about eighty-three more francs. I was naturally as delighted as I was surprised and rushed round to the Kodak shop to find that a lot of people at home send their films out here to be developed. That is an idea I propose to adopt.

I went from the Kodak shop to the Hôtel Eden to tell the Hunts that as Imogen and Jill were sick we would not drink with them that night.

I got into conversation with a man from Sussex who told me that my Westinghouse field-glasses were very cheap at 180 francs as they are part of the issue to G.I.s and sold by them on the black market.

So quite unwittingly I had achieved a bargain.

Somebody told me (this is apropos of nothing in particular) that the waitresses and shop-assistants get restive at this time of year because their fathers are often peasant-proprietors, and they are anxious to get back to the farms and vineyards.

To return to the subject of money. I had spent in all some two hundred to two hundred and fifty pounds in a fortnight for four of us. How did those undergraduates manage to come back at Christmas with more money than they took out? I was the richer not only in spirit and in bodily health but materially by a Parker pen, a calfskin brief-case, a pair of field-glasses and some excellent books, but it had been an expensive holiday. I wouldn't have missed it for anything in the world, for it had been easily the most enjoyable that I can ever remember.

I felt an entirely different person. My heart was troublesome and I got very tired, but in my spirit I felt a sense of exhilaration that I don't remember ever to have felt before.

On taking out my Revelation case to pack I found that the whole of the back framework had been smashed in. Rudolph the hall porter told me that I couldn't claim on this in spite of having insured my baggage because I had failed to report it on my arrival.

The children spent some time buying presents for their school-friends. They were inclined to go for scarves but I induced them to take playing-cards, because of their superiority to those which we get in England.

We walked home along the water-front which now grows daily intoxicatingly more beautiful. There were flowers all the way—wallflowers all along the low sea wall, beds of pansies and tulips in the gardens, magnolia trees and cherry trees in full blossom, and yellowy-green weeping willows shading the sunny way where children and American soldiers cycle in spite of notices (in English) to say that cycling is forbidden. We stopped to watch men and girls in shorts playing tennis and some visitors from the hotel rowing on the lake, a cheap pastime which costs only 1 fr. 50 c. per hour.

I went on alone to the Taverne du Château de Chillon where I carried on a mild flirtation with Hilda, who conveyed to me the fact that she would cry at our departure. It must be difficult to make love to a girl if neither of you can speak the other's language. A Swiss man at the next table raised his hat to me as he got up to go and said, "*Bon jour, monsieur.*"

I basked in the sun watching the passing traffic of splendid shining cars and shouting at intervals, "*Eelda, Eelda, encore du Campari,*" and when the smiling Hilda replenished my glass I would raise it each time and say "Cheero" and she would laugh and reply "Cheerio." It is the only word in English, if it is English, that she knows. I couldn't make her say "Cheero." It had to be "Cheerio."

When I got back to the Bonivard I found both Lalage and Imogen sitting on the terrace in the sun drying their hair which they had just washed. None of us had a bath for a fortnight as I dislike paying a franc for a bath. Lalage was in the throes of trying to condense Macaulay, and tearing her still wet hair in the process.

I went off to ask Rudolph about my suggested stroll for the afternoon down from Glion through the Gorge des Chaudrants. To my surprise he warned me against it.

"It is very steep," he said, "and the banisters are all gone." That made me all the more determined to try it.

I found at luncheon that I had been paying three francs a bottle for Evian water while the red wine named St. Georges was only 3 frs. 50 c. So I ordered a bottle of that only to discover that the St. Georges was not the one at Clarens, but in France. It was an inferior wine.

After lunch we walked to Territet station and caught the 1.55 funicular. The journey to Glion only takes eight minutes and cost 5 fr. 50 c. for the four of us, but as we sat in the rear seat overlooking the precipice I felt it cheap at the price, for it is a most thrilling experience. The line runs sheer up a vast precipice for two thousand feet and on either side are gardens with lilac trees and chestnuts in full bloom.

At Glion I took them through the Grand Hotel gardens to the terrace where we got a magnificent view of the lake. We were then misdirected and found ourselves in the grounds of a lyceum or boys' school. On retracing our steps towards the Bellevue we saw a wicket-gate on the right-hand side of the road and a notice: MONTREUX. SENTIR RAPIDE. *Rapide* is right. We started descending steps with an innumerable number of hairpin bends.

"Will you bet me that there are more than fifty?" asked Imogen.

"I won't," I said. "But I'll bet you that there are more than a thousand steps."

I could find no takers. I should, I think, have won.

For the next thirty-five minutes we jolted our stomachs and sweated in the sun descending steps.

Rudolph was right. There were no banisters.

Rudolph was wrong. It wasn't in the least dangerous.

We encountered an old woman talking to herself as she looked for wild flowers with which the wooded sides of the precipitous rocks were crowded.

Imogen gave me a gentian for my buttonhole. Jill complained of the steps. Lalage made me test her knowledge of *Pride and Prejudice*. I saw a black squirrel, the first I have ever seen.

At the foot of the gorge I saw a pleasant track going up the foot of the gully past the huge power-station. It bore a notice : CHEMIN DES GORGES INTERDIT TRAVAUX.

It was the only TRESPASSERS WILL BE PROSECUTED notice that I had seen in Switzerland. We emerged at Pallens, an old part of the town, and turned aside past a school out of which small girls in vivid blue frocks came running to the pump to explore the Temple, a noble tall-spired church built on a rock with a wide terrace overlooking the lake and the Rhône valley. The interior was disappointing. The mural paintings are modern and crude, but the views from the terrace more than compensate for that. I saw a memorial bust to a very fine-looking man called Doyen Brider, who had been pastor of Basle from 1786 to 1796, at Château d'Oex from 1796 to 1805, and at Montreux from 1805 to 1845. He was the author of *Du Conservateur Suisse*. Switzerland is not rich in authors.

The high walls above the road were gay with yellow rock-plants.

We descended a steep street and passed the only impoverished-looking man whom I had seen in Switzerland. He was unshaven, a dwarf, and wore a battered straw-hat.

By chance and great good fortune we elected to have tea at a *boulangerie* just opposite the fountain in the street facing the market-square. It was crowded with English visitors who were all enjoying banana-splits at 1 fr. 60 c. We began by sharing one and soon found that we needed another. Jill complained of a headache, but her sickness had disappeared. Imogen was her normal self, and in addition to the banana-split shared a strawberry cream-ice with me. I drank tea, the children Coca-cola, and Jill ate two meringues. Imogen added a doughnut. The whole bill including service came to 6 frs. 96 c. It was the cheapest tea we had had in Switzerland and by far the best.

The family were enjoying themselves hugely watching the passing crowds, composed mainly of obvious English people, which led two passers-by to say, "Horrible English types," and partly of smartly dressed pretty young Swiss girls. Two nurses in uniform trundled past pushing a low Swiss pram containing no fewer than seven babies in pink sunbonnets, all of the same age. They were remarkably urbane and well behaved.

Small boys carrying large satchels on their backs passed quickly on their way home from school.

"I love this place," said Lalage.

Jill suddenly decided to buy a lot of cigarettes as presents.

I suddenly felt that the Alps were slipping from my grasp. I got up.

"You must learn to handle the Swiss currency for yourself," I said. "I'm going down to the water-front."

Disregarding all pleas to stay and not to be selfish I left them, and went down to the lakeside to look out on the snowy peaks and listen to the lapping of the waves, which were quite high.

I had now achieved my place in the sun. The shops were all shrouded in yellow sunblinds. I watched a black kite swoop down from the sky, disperse the gulls and neatly scoop up a shining fish in its talons from the surface of the water. I watched three American soldiers cycle dangerously and awkwardly up and down the forbidden promenade. I smelt the wallflowers. I was well content to wait till the family had finished their shopping. A rowing-boat newly painted dark blue outside and light blue inside passed close to the shore.

The family returned and to their surprise I suggested buying tickets for the nearby Apollo.

"What on earth's coming over you?" said Jill. "You know that wild horses won't drag you to the flicks."

"This," I retorted, "is different. It's Swiss. It's called *Menschen*-something."

"What does that mean?" asked Imogen.

"I haven't the faintest idea, but it's German-Swiss. I didn't know there was a Swiss film. I've an idea that it'll be good."

My family need no recommendation to any film. They are catholic in their taste.

We booked our seats, the smiling woman refusing our vouchers, as usual, and we then walked for the second time that day the whole length of the water-front to Chillon. It was indescribably pleasant in the soft afternoon light. I saw a white and red frock in the water, a sure sign in England that the woman had committed suicide. In Switzerland I doubt whether anyone ever commits suicide. I didn't worry.

The path became less and less frequented.

On the bridge at Chillon a lovely young girl with glistening fair hair stood smiling down at me. I waved up to her and she waved down at me. Nearer contact was not sought by either of us. We were two lovers of the blue water and the white hills who needed no language to express what was in our hearts.

I sat in the sun outside the Taverne with the smiling Hilda hovering above me and waited for my family. A neatly dressed and very good-looking young man sat at the next table. He told me that he was educated at Summerfields, Lancing, and Christ's. I told him my name. He delighted me by remembering the name of one of my novels.

" I quite enjoyed it," he said.

" You surprise me," I replied.

" I was only fifteen," he said apologetically.

" That explains it," I said, and added " When you were green in judgment."

He spoke perfect French, so he was able to act as interpreter between Hilda and myself.

She seemed surprised to find that I was an English author.

" Tell her that I'm not in the least like Byron," I said. " I don't want there to be any misunderstanding."

The laughter that followed was prolonged. I was not conscious of having perpetrated a joke.

The young man told me that he was employed at the Palace Hotel.

" I thought the Swiss disliked giving the foreigner a job."

" They do. But they like to get jobs in England. I'm an exchanged hostage."

I found it almost impossible to leave my bedroom window to go down to dinner. The whole room was flooded with sunlight and there was the usual evening kaleidoscopic performance of the setting sun.

"The hills are the colour of very dark grapes," said Jill.

" If only you could do the writing," I said.

The film was even better than I expected. The house, a small one, was only half-full. The Swiss are not filmgoers.

The characters had all got human faces. I felt that they were personalities off the stage. The story was simple.

We were shown a travelling circus arriving in a remote market-town in the mountains. The heroine, daughter of the proprietor, who rode a bicycle on a tight-rope, left the circus to his great indignation to marry a very pleasant farmer. The pull of the circus is too much for her when it comes again on its circuit a year later. She goes to see her father who falls off his tight-rope and is killed. The circus is about to be broken up when she decides, in spite of her love for her husband, to return to it and so save it from disintegration.

The film was in German and there were no French captions. I gathered from the laughter that it was witty. It was certainly moving, and the acting was as natural as the photography was superb.

It was I think the most satisfying film that I have ever seen.

The only trouble was my inability to keep my eyes open. I have seldom endured such agony trying to keep awake.

I think I was asleep on this night before my head touched the pillow.

Friday, 25th April, 1947

It was a clear and cloudless dawn but the birds didn't begin to sing much before five o'clock.

I spent rather more time than I could afford standing at the open window taking my last dawn look at the Alps.

Even then I couldn't believe that they were real. Beauty lies in the eye of the beholder. Did those stumpy, ugly, chattering little English secondary-school girls that went running past the Bonivard down to the tram see what I saw? Did the white-haired solitary old English ladies staying in the Bonivard see what I saw?

And what, because I am only an average prose writer, did Shelley and Byron see?

I can't believe that the vision vouchsafed to them was lovelier than the vision vouchsafed to me.

I felt suffused, radiant, transfigured.

It was, I knew, only partly the Alps. It was also the wine, the food, the friendliness, the cleanliness, the novelty, the sun, the blue sky, the blue water, the warmth and the all-round efficiency. Everything works in Switzerland. The trains run to time and are fast. The only thing I didn't like was the Hoover which buzzed round the lounge at 7.30 every morning when I was trying to work.

Rudolph translated the title of the film for me. It is called *Menschen Die Verüberzieher* (Men who wander about).

He also told me that the Swiss customs allow no gold or material to be taken out of the country, but permit the taking of two kilograms of clothes, and two kilograms of food (chocolates, cheese, etc.) so long as it is carried in the hand-baggage.

Herr Boenski gave me my hotel bill after breakfast. It came to a hundred and fifty-one francs. As none of us had had a bath for a fortnight that represents wine and early morning tea. The tea costs seventy centimes a time. That means that I spent about eight pounds on wine and seven pounds on Campari and other aperitifs during my stay, an average of a pound a day on drinks. I don't regret it. I'm merely stating the fact. I'd spent about a pound a day on cigars. I don't regret that either. When you're having a bust, go the whole hog.

Entirely without calculating I had just made my money last out, which means that my all-in expenses for the sixteen days for the four of us came to just £230—say £250 with the expenses in England. I call the holiday cheap at the price. This includes frock, shoes, shoulder-bag, bathing-costume, purse, socks and a six-coloured pencil for Imogen; shoes, sun-glasses, socks, bathing-costume, pack of cards and watch-strap for Lalage; shoes, skiing-jersey, skiing-cap, bathing-costume, socks, stockings, gloves and diary for Jill; and for myself one hundred cigars, notebook, diary, purse, brief-case, field-glasses, handkerchiefs, writing-blocks, Parker pen, silver snuffbox, pocket-knife, six-coloured pencil, fifteen rolls of film, a print of Chillon, hair-brush, sponge, and seven quite expensive books on Switzerland.

Jill had to go home without the ring (forty-eight francs) that she so much coveted.

"Next time I shan't drink," she said.

"Next time I shall drink more," I retaliated.

I had now got rid of all my vouchers and had only a hundred francs left, twenty of which would have to go on registering the baggage and thirty-six on the developed films. I was running it too fine.

I got into conversation with two typical Bonivardian middle-aged English ladies.

We talked of families. They seemed to be related to most of the old aristocracy. It was like listening to my mother. How I used to despise her for her snobbery. How she would have hated the modern England, and how right she would have been to hate it.

It is a pity that Socialism is so completely concerned with material benefits.

It is grand to think that most people are getting material comfort. It is appalling to think of the cost in the loss of spiritual and aesthetic values.

Boenski gave me a *bon* to buy cheese without coupons, so Imogen and I had a merry half-hour in a Territet dairy choosing cheeses.

I selected a Limburger, forgetting its pungent smell, a Gruyère, and others that looked like Dutch. I spent seven francs.

Sadly we made our way for the last time to the Taverne to say au revoir to Hilda.

I found that she had on a new uniform, a blouse of (*grège* she called it) oyster silk, a tiny apron of green and white, and a very short brown skirt.

Two American G.I.s, with pale and rather tawdry wives and four appalling children, sat at the next table. They were from Wiesbaden, and told us that the Germans in their area were certainly getting enough to eat. When they gave the children candy they took it away not to eat but to sell in the Black Market. They told us all sorts of interesting things which I couldn't listen to with undivided attention as the most loathsome of the four children, a boy of three dressed as a G.I. in full uniform with a pipe in his mouth and wearing sun-glasses, kept on shouting out "Squirt" to Lalage and Imogen. He was not, as I at first imagined, asking them to use the soda syphon.

I tried to guess the States from which the families came.

One was from Texas, the other Alabama.

They were certainly "poor whites."

One thing I did hear that startled me. The Germans apparently are hoping to join up with us against the Russians.

In the meanwhile they are waging a quiet war of nerves.

"The telephone's always ringing," said one of the American wives, "and an unknown voice says 'Did you know that your boy has just been run over?' or 'Do you know that your husband is running around with some girl?'"

Lalage formed, on the strength of this encounter, an unfortunate view of the Americans.

"I think they're common," she said.

I could hear my mother's voice.

I found out, to my surprise, that these unprepossessing families were staying in Montreux's luxury hotel.

"They feed us," said one of the wives, "worse than we are fed at Wiesbaden."

For the moment I forgot that the Americans get all their food, as well as their clothes, sent over from the States.

I got a considerable jolt when Hilda asked if I would give her fellow waitress a drink. She had been making signs at me for a long time which I could not interpret. It made me realise how much in common the Swiss have with the French.

I shouldn't say that Hilda is grasping, because she has always been reluctant to take the franc tip that I give her each morning and night.

We left the hotel at two o'clock. I avoided saying good-bye to anybody, but the maids came to the window and waved us away.

We drove to the station well loaded. There were four cases to be registered, and between us we carried seven more and a rug.

Rudolph went off to register the four big pieces. The cost was sixteen francs. I gave him a pound for himself and then had to borrow ten francs from him for the journey.

The platform was crowded. I picked up a paper and read to my astonishment of 88-miles-an-hour gales in England and of *Warspite* going aground off the Cornish coast.

All the couriers sorted out their parties, and at 3.18 we set off in a very comfortable through carriage for Basle.

I gazed out on the lake and the mountains all the way to Lausanne, where I found to my delight that we were taking a new route to Basle by way of Neuchâtel.

The country through which we ran was rather like Sussex. It

was gentle, undulating, and well cultivated, with a good deal of plough. Then we ran through a wide plain of black alluvial exactly like the fen country. It was hedgeless and full of dykes. It was different from the fens in its number of vast castles and monasteries perched up on knolls.

At Yverdon we came to the south side of Lake Neuchâtel and thereafter ran along the west bank of that enchanting lake, with vineyards growing on the lower slopes and trees growing on the steep sides of the limestone range on our left. Across the lake we got an amazing panorama of the whole of the Alpine peaks from the Jungfrau to Mont Blanc. It was quite unbelievable and quite unforgettable. The whole of the eastern horizon was taken up by these snow-clad peaks. In the very centre rose one isolated titanic rock that was completely devoid of snow. It was easy to pick out the Dent du Midi and the mountains behind Montreux, just as it was easy to pick out the Eiger, Mönch and Jungfrau. But the others defeated me. I just gazed and gazed over the still shining waters to the great heights.

I was not surprised to see how handsome were the houses built on the lakeside that enjoyed this wonderful view.

At Neuchâtel we saw the castle but no sign of the famous falls.

We left this lake only to run along the banks of a smaller one, that of Bienne, where I saw the Omega watch factory. We then entered a tunnel which took six minutes to negotiate and emerged at Montier in a quite different but very lovely country, all high limestone rocks and narrow defiles. I at last saw the justice of Byron's comment on Matlock, "The Switzerland of England." This was exactly like the country through which the train runs between Chinley and Cromford.

Houses now became more frequent, and more and more people boarded the train at the stops. We were approaching Basle by way of clean attractive suburbs rich in orchards.

We reached Basle at seven o'clock, and as the train for Calais was not due to leave till eleven o'clock we looked forward to a good dinner and a stroll down to the Rhine.

But it didn't pan out like that. Lunn's representative met us and told us to have dinner in the station buffet and then immediately join the queue for the passports examination. That struck me as crazy.

"There are over a thousand people going through tonight," he said.

Our dinner consisted of soup, a generous helping of fish, and an ice and cost 4 frs. 50 c. each. I was reduced to drinking lager and had nothing left over to buy rolls and butter and brandy for the night journey. An Englishman asked me to change a franc for 1s. 2d. He little knew that it was almost my last franc.

We joined the queue in the chocolate and fruit stall on the station where we found oranges being sold at eightpence each. The woman behind the counter was as surly as if she had been English.

I kept on losing sight of Jill or Imogen or Lalage. I suddenly felt very tired and lost my temper.

"Next time," I said, "I shall come out alone."

"We shall all be glad about that," said Jill, and walked out of the station. It took me so long to recover her that when we got back to the station we were far back in a queue that seemed to go on for ever.

Lalage found a school-friend and became oblivious of everyone else. Jill cursed all queues and told me to go off and get some brandy. My heart was behaving very oddly.

"I have no money left for brandy," I said. "I have no money left at all."

We stood like cattle in a solid phalanx for over an hour. There was no sign of any customs officer or passport examiner.

Then Lunn's man came along and said that he had secured a place for us further up the line.

"I don't want to get lynched," I said wearily, "I'm staying where I am."

He seemed stunned by my stupidity.

"You don't know the English," I said.

When eventually we started to move I felt that my heart would give way altogether, for we had to shuffle along, picking up and putting down our bags at one-yard intervals. It was an appalling and wholly unnecessary experience. It would surely be easy to have ten passport examiners instead of one.

We came to a place where it was possible to put the bags on a shining metal barrier or counter which ran parallel with our course, and here everyone fought for a place by its side in order

F

to push the bags along instead of picking them up and putting them down every thirty seconds.

Always in future I shall have a porter. But, then, I had no Swiss money.

Imogen looked pale and wan. I was giddy, and my heart was pumping ferociously. Jill was angry and Lalage taciturn. It was a merry party.

At last we shuffled past the passport man and were ushered like cattle into a huge waiting-room. The train had not come in. When the barriers were opened we rushed like a tide-bore through the opening onto the platform and scurried like rabbits for our seats. There were two trains. The one on our right was the sleeping-car train. As we all had reserved seats the rush seemed unnecessary.

To my complete surprise Lunn's man came back and said, "Never mind about your seats. Come to the front of the train."

In a mystified daze we followed and found ourselves ushered into a very uncomfortable compartment in a train even dirtier than an English one.

"You won't be disturbed here," he said optimistically.

We tried to settle down. Imogen fell asleep almost as soon as we put her legs up. Lalage couldn't get comfortable, and said so very often.

Hours seemed to pass. We watched the sleeping-car train move out half-empty.

"We ought to have gone on that," I said.

I turned the lights off. I settled down to sleep. For a time all was quiet. Then people began to walk up and down the corridor and peer in. I put a scarf over my head and refused to look or listen.

Then to my surprise the door opened and the courier from a rival agency, without any by your leave, turned on the light and said, "I've got to have seats."

He was, I felt, no good advertisement for English courtesy. He went away leaving the light on and the door open. I soon remedied that.

At eleven o'clock we pulled out.

We still had the compartment to ourselves.

I RETURN TO SWITZERLAND

I SLEPT well. I woke to see grey skies. There was a high wind and it was cold. We were in France. I looked out on a dull, flat, impoverished countryside.

The transition was so abrupt that I felt like Lucifer suddenly evicted from Heaven and finding it difficult to reconcile himself to Hell.

Lunn's man came in about 5.30 and recommended us to go along to breakfast at once.

"You'll find a queue already," he said.

We did. We passed compartment after compartment of gross-looking, sleepy and tired tourists. I thought of washing. The lavatories were foul, without water, soap, towels or toilet-paper. I thought better of trying to wash. We joined the queue and stood in an appalling draught for nearly an hour.

Then those who had breakfasted squeezed past, not with the look of repletion of the well-fed but grumbling.

"Appalling," they said. "No milk, no butter. So foul we couldn't eat it. Rook you like hell."

"Shall we go back?" said Jill.

"Not on your life," I said.

We remained to be pleasantly surprised.

There was a large cup of black coffee which was hot. There were rusks and a little jam. The cost for that was 1s. 6d. Jill, Imogen and I had a fried egg and bacon. That cost 4s. each. It struck me as reasonable. The waiters were not as rude as I expected French waiters to be.

I looked out on the desolate grey landscape.

"Where's Rheims?" asked Imogen. "I want to see the jack-daw."

"You'll see no bird in France," I said. "They shoot 'em."

"Poor things," said Imogen.

We passed through Laon at 7.10.

"We've missed Rheims," I said.

Lalage suddenly woke up. She had seen some bread. She adores bread.

As I had a hundred French francs I made her pay her bill herself. It came to 34 frs. 70 c. Ours came to 384 frs. 50 c.

"I hope," said Lalage, "they take French money."

"It is not," I said, "unusual in France."

"This is the first time I've drunk out of a chipped cup for a fortnight," said Jill.

We fought our way back to the carriage through a queue that seemed to extend the whole length of the train. We then joined the queue for the lavatory.

I transferred my few remaining Swiss coins from my purse to my waistcoat pocket and put French coins in my pocket-book.

At 10.30 we passed through Boulogne and saw sand-dunes and smelt the sea.

"I'm glad I'm an islander," I said.

My family gaped at me open-mouthed.

"You're glad?" said Jill.

"Glad," I repeated.

"Turncoat," said Imogen.

We joined the queue in the corridor to leave the train early. I stood for an hour quite pointlessly, for when the train drew into Calais the door was locked and we had to go the other way.

As the English travellers drew nearer home they got tougher and ruder.

We joined a Rugger scrum which would have done justice to any 'varsity side.

I have no hesitation at all in awarding the palm for roughness to the Polytechnic. They used elbows. They shouted. They fought. They used their weight. They got through with flying colours. They were not popular.

We eventually reached the deck of the boat more or less unscathed. The fact that I was bleeding was due, not to the Polytechnic, but to the fact that I had squashed my little finger shutting the carriage window.

I found an extremely attentive English sailor who secured four deck-chairs for us on which we placed our bags and rugs and then went down to take our place in the queue for lunch. We were lucky. When the doors opened we were counted. I was No. 51 and admitted to the first service.

I ate an unexpectedly good luncheon of cold meat. I drank gin and beer. I paid in English money. I was again rich. I had nearly eighty pound notes in my pocket.

We were given yellow landing-tickets and listened to a voice on the loudspeaker giving instructions in all languages.

England apparently makes it difficult for the foreigner to land. Why he comes over I can't think.

We climbed on deck just in time to see the last of Calais. England looked only a step away. There was a fresh north wind, but the sun was shining. It was as calm as could be.

"You should have been with us yesterday," said my sailor-friend. "The waves came over the funnel. Robert Newton was with us. He was in *Temptation Harbour*. They laid the scene for that in Folkestone."

He pointed to a ship rapidly approaching.

"That's the *Invicta*. First-class only. Four thousand tons. She crosses in under the hour. Fifty-nine minutes. The *Golden Arrow* boat. She's a treat. But she rolls. No top deck as we have. All cabins. She's a thousand tons heavier than us."

He told me the story of *Warspite* and of the lifeboat that was sunk with all hands yesterday.

Lalage went off to talk to a school-friend. Lunn's man told me to join the queue for disembarking. I was tired of joining queues and disregarded his advice.

I ran into Arnold Lunn who was responsible for my original visit to Switzerland twenty-five years ago. I had not seen him since. He looked incredibly young.

"You're writing about Switzerland I suppose?" he asked.

"Yes."

"You might let me 'vet' what you write. Then there'd be a chance of you getting something accurate."

"I've not forgotten," I said, "that I haven't yet had you up for libel for making me the villain of your novel *Loose Ends*. I'll let you 'vet' my book instead."

"That's a bargain," he said. "And before you write anything, you'd better read my book, *Switzerland and the English*."

"Too late," I said, "my book's practically written."

I have a deep affection for Arnold Lunn and a great respect for his intelligence.

I did not hurry off the boat, but I was glad to put my foot on English soil again.

We boarded the first train quickly owing to the efficient help of Lunn's man. This time I had the good sense to have a porter. It seemed to ease my passage a lot.

We easily found seats that had not been reserved and immediately joined the queue for tea.

The compartment was comfortable, the tea (for England) little short of staggering. There was buttered toast, bread, jam, sandwiches, cake and lashings of tea to drink. It cost 2s. 6d. a head. I looked out on the sweet Kent scene. There were young lambs everywhere. The orchards were in full bloom. Cowslips lined the embankment.

"The houses look solid and the country old," said Jill.

I looked at the anemones that carpeted the woods.

"It's cosy," I said.

We looked out on a green field with men in white flannels running to and fro. "Cricket," said Lalage. "How lovely."

"Wizard," said Imogen. It was the first time she had used the word since leaving Montreux.

We saw people playing football, bowls, tennis and also bathing.

This was our England.

We arrived at Victoria to find that it was double summertime and already five o'clock.

I was lucky in my porter.

The customs officer looked genial. He handed me a board with writing on it. I felt as if I were at the oculist's.

I read that I was expected to declare everything, worn or not worn.

I pointed to my field-glasses and brief-case, rather proudly, feeling extraordinarily self-righteous.

"Secondhand," I said.

"How much?" said he.

"Eight pounds the one and nine pounds the other," I said.

He worked something out on paper, took the number of my field-glasses and then nearly took my breath away by saying,

"Thirteen pounds three and fourpence."

I was glad that I was so well equipped with pound notes.

I suppose I ought to have asked him how he arrived at that figure, but as other passengers were having their possessions strewn all over the counter and he was marking all my eleven cases with chalk without examination I felt that it would be more discreet to keep silent.

I wonder what the other passengers were made to pay.

As we emerged single-file through the barrier Imogen said,
"Next time I'm going to bring my own chalk and mark them myself."

"You'll have to bring a thousand coloured chalks," said Lalage. "This time it's mauve."

An enormous crowd of sightseers had come to welcome us home.

"I feel like a film-star," said Imogen.

"I feel like something in the Zoo," said Lalage.

An old pupil of mine emerged from the crowd.

We went in search of a taxi.

I took the registered bulky luggage to Paddington. Jill took the children and the small stuff to the Milestone Hotel.

With considerable misgiving I left my brief-case with all my precious manuscript, glasses and camera at the Great Western Hotel, and was then driven quickly across Hyde Park, where all London seemed to be sunning itself, to rejoin my family at the Milestone.

I found Jill in a palatial room overlooking Kensington Gardens.

"I'm taking the children to the Round Pond," I said.

"What a lot of dogs," said Imogen as we ran over the rough grass towards the lake.

"What a lot of yachts," said Lalage. "Who sails them?"

An old white-haired man in yachting-shoes, holding a long pole, ran past.

"The very old," I said, "and the very young."

It was a lovely sight. Wild duck flew over and sank to rest among the white sails. Small boys fished while lovers looked on. Nursemaids wheeled their charges past. It was hot. It was sunny. It was London in the spring. It was well-nigh perfect.

We went back to the Milestone and found that the head waiter was a native of Montreux.

We dined off melon, chicken and junket.

It was Cup Tie Final night, so when we got to the New Victoria we found it packed out. We went off to the Grosvenor for coffee, and returned at 8.30 to find seats at 3s. 6d. for *Temptation Harbour*.

This admirable film excited the children because they once more saw the Folkestone that they had so recently left.

Simenon's story had been twisted to suit the cinema-goers' taste, but it was good for all that, and I stayed awake easily.

I noticed that the British cinema-goer is much more emotional than the Swiss. There was quite a lot of applause.

That night I had my first bath for fifteen days.

Sunday, 27th April, 1947

I was up as usual at four and the first birds began to sing in Kensington Gardens at 5.55. That would be 4.55 in Montreux.

It was a quiet cloudless dawn with a touch of ground-frost. I breakfasted at eight and encountered some champions of Burnley still in hot argument over the match.

"I suppose the better side won?" I said.

That was naughty of me. It took me a long time to escape.

At the hall door I met another group of five men and took it for granted that they were also Lancastrians in defeat.

"Going home sadder and poorer men?" I said.

"We're just going to fly to the Persian Gulf," said one of them in a strong Cockney accent.

Two long-bearded patriarchs in black frock-coats and black homburgs carrying umbrellas passed me.

London, I felt, is still cosmopolitan.

My bill for dinner, bed and breakfast for the four of us came to £5 10s.

The rest of the family breakfasted late and were kept waiting. There were no taxis. We had to trail our bags to Kensington High Street where we found a taxi to take us to the Great Western Hotel.

I was relieved to find my brief-case still intact.

We were told that the 10.10 for Oxford ran from No. 5 platform. It ran from No. 3.

In our carriage there was one taciturn woman who regarded us with such disfavour that I am sure she smelt the Limburger.

We went off for coffee as soon as the train left; and the taciturn lady left us at Reading.

We crossed the Thames at the Goring Gap.

"The land looks very rich," said Jill.

"Can you help me with my punctuation?" said Lalage.

It started to rain as we pulled into Oxford station.

"The spires still stand," said Jill.

"And the rain still falls," said Imogen.

As soon as we got inside our house I turned the wireless on.

I listened to recordings of the sedge-warblers. I went down to the pub for my morning beer. The children went off to collect their beloved Cairn, Simon.

We were home again, and, oddly enough, glad to be.

IMOGEN'S DIARY

Wednesday 9th April 1947. Sun

I WOKE up at 6.30 and, as I was feeling very exited (about going to Switzerland) turned the light on but to my dismay it was not time to get up. After another 1 hr I got up, dressed and began to pack, but as soon as I had got ¼ way mummy came in to help me.

After break-fast we took a taxi to the station and got on the 10.15. When we arrived in London it was only 12,0,clock, so we put our lugage in the milestone Hotel and went to lunch with Nevel and his girl friend and two of daddy's publishers. After lunch we went to a film called "The Man Within." It was lovely only not as good as the book. When we came out of that we went to a cocktail party. And then I went to bed.

Thursday 10th April 1947. Sun

AFTER having a very good break-fast we left the Milestone Hotel, took a taxi to the Grovnor, put our bagage down and went to "Bumpus" a book shop, where I bought a book called "The Turnings of the Shrew." Then after seeing Antonia at the London Clinic we went to have lunch. There was an orful que outside the Grovnor for customs when we came out. After that we had a pretty nice journey to Foxton and then we took a boat from Foxton to Caly, the boat hardly went up and down at all it was so carm. Then at Caly we had to have customs again and then after that we courght the train to Switzerland which was 1 hr late and had a lovely dinner in the Pullman.

Friday 11th April 1947. Sun

I HAD a very disturbed night and when I woke up it was 5.30. I tried to go to sleep again but it did not work so I looked at a map untill we got to Basle, and then we had a wonderful break-fast. When we had had break-fast we caught another train to Montreux. After another 4 or 5 hours we went into the Pullman to have lunch which consisted of about 6 corses. And as I was so full I took back an apple to eat in our carriage. Then, suddenly we saw the wonderful Alps shining in the distence with the sun pouring down on them, and then as suddenly as they had come they went and we were in Montreux Station. We took a taxi to the Bonivard Hotel, saw our rooms etc. and then went down to the town and bought some coclates *off the Ration*. Then we took a tram to the hotel, had super and went to bed.

Saturday 12th Aprill 1947. Sun

DURING break-fast daddy was phoned up, and came back saying that we had been envited to the last skiing day up in Gstaad. So after a very hurried break-fast we got on the train. It was a very nice journey only a bit frightening as we went over presapuses. The Alps on every side gliding past and everything was very still. At last we got to Gstaad and there was a lovely Pony and trap to meet us, we got in and we trotted right through the town untill we got to a Skihoist which is a seat which is hung up by a piece of Iron on a long wire and you are hauled up mountains in it. It was very frightening at first but lovely afterwards. When we got to the top we had lunch and then I took off my shoes and socks and sunbathed, while I whatched some people skiing. It was bliss running up and down on hot boards, but at last we had to go back. So we travelled down on the skihoist, trotted to the station and courght the train to Montreux.

14   *Sun*

I GOT up rather early, had break-fast and then waited outside on the terrace of the Bonivard Hotel for our Lunns man to come and pick us up as we were going to Gruiéres. We started $\frac{1}{4}$ of an hour late. It was wonderful hearing the lake rippeling past for about a mile and then we turned down the Rohne Valley which had the useual lovely scenery with bubeling streams and shinning Alps on every side. Aventually we came to a wayside café where we had 11ses. After that we went down a little to Gruéres where we lunch and we were showed round a very old castle with wonderful tapestry. Then we were let free to shop. We did not by anithing. Then on the way home we visited a cheese factory which smelt orful and then we went home.

15   Sun

WE ordered break-fast early at 8,0,clock to go for a ride to Geniva in a caribon. We started at 9.15, and went round all the Hotels to collect the people who were coming with us. And when we really started for Geniva it was an hour later. We passed through some tremendous vin-yards which had grapes just growing and then we stopped at Churchhills new house: When people had taken snaps of it we came to Geniva where the driver droped us and we eat our wonderful packed lunch which consisted of two meat rolls, one plain roll, one egg, one box of cheese, two oranges and a glass of frappé (milk shack). After lunch we went shopping and I bought a pair of shoes. But after that I saw some people bathing and then went home. And after super we went to a film called " The Right to Live."

16   Sun

IN the morning we went shopping and we all bought bathing costumes and then I suddenly saw a wonderful dolls shop which had wizard dolls that wogeld their eyes and had real long hair only I was pulled away by mummy saying that it was a waste of money. So after that we went to have daddys films developed and then we went home for lunch. In the afternoon we went to Naye. We started on a very very steep Fenicular and then we cought a train. When we got there the shiers came to meet us. Then we climbed the mountain but half way up daddy heart failed him so he had to come down as it was 6,000 ft up. Then I put on my bathing costume and ran about in that untill after tea when I had to put them on because the train was going. So we cought the train went down the fenicular and arrived at the Bonivard in time for super. And then after super we went for a walk.

17   *Sun*

I GOT up very late and it was 9.30 when we had all finished break-fast. Then we went down town to shop and after about 10 dress shops we found a very nice summer frock with blue flowers on for me. Then we went down to the front and had a milk-shack and then daddy took some photographs of us. In the afternoon we went to Champary, we passed over the Rohne and then we went up a very wigly steep road and as I was sitting just infront of the engin I was roasted. When we got there we had tea and then bought some post-cards and then we went home. When we arrive a man had arrive that was going to have super with us, so we had super and went to bed.

Sun

IN the morning we went shopping and daddy bought 2 note books and mummy bought a slicer, Lal a pair of shoes and me a heart purse than daddy got some pictures he had taken of us. In the afternoon I went up to Les Avants by train and walked down to Montreux. First of all we went into a shop and then we began to descend the hill to Glion. On the way I picked some lovely flowers of all kinds and I had got about 18 differant wild flowers by the time I got to Glion then we had tea and then we walked to the Bonivard had super and went to a film " Les Ailes blanches."

18   **Sun**

IN the morning we shoped and we bourght a white pullover, cigars, a pen, note book and a lovely heart purse (sorry this is the wrong day), a skiing cap, shoes, print of Chillon castle and a lovely bag. In the afternoon we went to Lausan and climbed a very steep hill to the " Old India " where we were going to have tea. After a most dellishous ice we courght the train home and then went to a film "Tonight and Everynight."

19   **Sun**

IN the morning we went to a Catholic church and the surmon was all in Latin and French. But the church itself had two beautiful Angels standing behind the altar. What amased me most was that there 2 collections, one by an old man of about 90 and the other by a woman of 50. Then we went to Chillon by the lake side and after that we had lunch. In the afternoon we went with our bathing costumes hopefully to Montreux Plage but there was nobody bathing. So we cought the Steamer to St Gingolf and had tea on it then we went back to Chillon and had a drink at the Cavern. Then after super we went out with Mr Alblas and came back at about 11,0,clock.

20   *Sun*

IN the morning I shopped and daddy bought a lovely brief case which he had cheaper because it was sunburnt. Then we collected some pictures of us all which came out very well. After that we took Lalage's shoe to the menders and the sole was put on while we waited. In the Afternoon we went to Villars and I had to sit infront with Wety while he made wet jokes. When we got there we saw some soldiers singing songs on a bank. And then we collided with some other people of our group and had tea with them. In the midle of tea my tooth came out. Then mummy bought a pair of socks and somebody bought me a mouse called Hilda. On the way home looking down on the Rohne valley was lovely. When we reached the cavern we stopped to have a drink and then went home to dinner.

21st April   *Sun*

IN the morning we got up very early had break-fast and then went to catch a taxi outside our hotel. When we got to the station we suddenly saw Rogie a girl at my last school. Then when both our families had met we got into a carriage and we talked about how other people were and when they got here etc. After talking for a while we got out of the train and went down hill to the Blue Lake where there were a lot of fish. The Lake was a wonderful transparent culler and you could see the bottom quite easily. Then we had lunch and went to have a drink at a restrant but as soon as we had started drinking a man came along and told us that there was only three more minutes before the train went so we gulped down our orange sqash and rushed up the hill towards the train. When we got there we only just got in before it started. After a tunel of about 15 minutes and a lot of little stations we arrived at Interlarken where we shopped and Mr Hunt bourght me a packet of chocolates.

BIBLIOGRAPHY

1. SWITZERLAND, by Doré Ogrizek and J. G. Rufenacht. (B.O.R. Zurich, 18 frs.) A very gaily coloured and extremely informative interpretation of the Swiss scene which is indispensable.

2. LA HAUTE ROUTE, by André Roch. (Jean Marguerat, Lausanne, 20 frs.) Seventy-seven magnificent full-page photographs of Chamonix, Zermatt and Saas-Fee.

3. LES ALPES, by Hans Schmithat. (Fretz Frères S.A., Zurich, 30 frs.) Three hundred and twenty superb photographs, several of them coloured, of the High Alps.

4. SWITZERLAND AND THE ENGLISH, by Arnold Lunn. (Eyre and Spottiswoode, 15/-.)

5. SWITZERLAND IN ENGLISH PROSE AND POETRY, edited by Arnold Lunn. (Eyre and Spottiswoode, 16/-.)

6. SWITZERLAND. The Traveller's Illustrated Guide. (Faber and Faber, 18/-.)

7. SWITZERLAND, by Arnold Lunn. (Harrap, 5/-.)

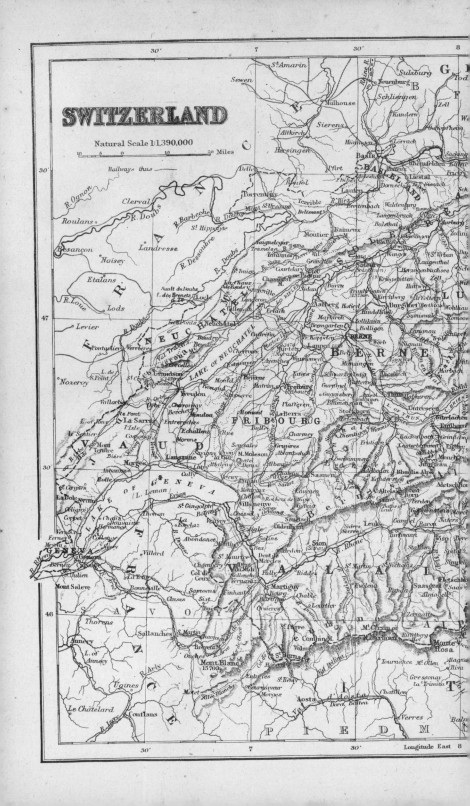

SWITZERLAND

Natural Scale 1:1,390,000

10 5 0 10 20 Miles

Railways thus